ADVANCES IN CANCER IMMUNOTHERAPY

ADVANCES IN CANCER IMMUNOTHERAPY

From Serendipity to Cure

HONJO Tasuku

Translated by Andrew Gonzalez

Japan Publishing Industry Foundation for Culture

Note on Romanization
This book follows the Hepburn system of romanization. For proper nouns and terms with official romanizations, the official romanizations are used even if they do not follow Hepburn style. Except for citations and references to works that were published with macrons, the use of macrons has been omitted from the text. Long vowels in reference citations are rendered as single letters rather than double letters, except for "ei." The tradition of placing the family name first has been followed for Japanese names.

Advances in Cancer Immunotherapy: From Serendipity to Cure
Honjo Tasuku. Translated by Andrew Gonzalez.

Published by
Japan Publishing Industry Foundation for Culture (JPIC)
2-2-30 Kanda-Jinbocho, Chiyoda-ku, Tokyo 101-0051, Japan

First English edition: March 2021

This book is a translation of *Gan men'ekiryoho towa nanika* published by Iwanami Shoten, Publishers, Tokyo in 2019.
English publishing rights arranged with Iwanami Shoten, Publishers, Tokyo.

Book design: Miki Kazuhiko, Ampersand Works

Printed in Japan
ISBN 978-4-86658-176-7
https://japanlibrary.jpic.or.jp/

CONTENTS

PREFACE TO THE ENGLISH EDITION

COVID-19: A Revealing Window on the Significance of Science

The significance and value of science can be hard to see.

When the economy is down, science is a prime target for public budget cuts. Investments in science do not produce results right away. It takes years or decades of research to nurture something that can bear major fruit for return to the world. In many cases, useful results never come. However, it is from multitudes of such studies that breakthroughs emerge.

By one year after the publication of the original Japanese edition of this book in April 2019, the COVID-19 pandemic had spread to every corner of the globe. The pandemic is an opportunity for people to recognize the significance and value of science through real-life experience. Battles with infections are protracted fights, and no one can predict when a new infection will arise. It is absolutely critical to determine how to prevent infection with timely quarantines. It would not be an overstatement to say that using quarantines to stave off infections is a matter of national defense. Before an infection breaks out and enters the country, it is necessary to designate who will spearhead the response and who will be responsible for arranging healthcare personnel, personal protective equipment, and medication. As of July 2020, it seems that Japan's COVID-19 response is being spearheaded by the National Institute of Infectious Diseases. However, it is nearly impossible to ascertain how much authority they have actually been given. Just because someone possesses a medical license does not mean they can effectively combat infections. Perhaps the only organization in Japan that has successfully handled COVID-19 is the Self-Defense Forces, due to their daily training and leadership.

In the context of infections, not all scientists say the same thing. Scientists' statements reflect their fields of expertise and their bodies of research. Unsurprisingly, non-scientists can become confused, not knowing which scientists' statement to believe as true. Scientists must take great care in how they deliver their messages, being mindful of how much evidence supports their statement. Also, scientists' statements regarding what will happen with an infection and how much it will spread are merely projections. Because there are far too many factors that affect the spread of an infection, it is impossible for a prediction to convince everyone. Our ability to predict the future is limited. When scientists make statements, they must present sufficient evidence and carefully explain that their estimates are based on hypotheses derived from that evidence. Otherwise, scientists will end up simply showing a bunch of numbers and confusing most people. In addition, scientists' explanations must be consistent and coherent. If the gist of scientists' statements does not match their past statements, people will stop believing those scientists.

How unfortunate it is for people to stop believing scientists.

To repeat myself, scientists must clearly convey in their statements where the evidence ends and where the estimation begins. It is also important for scientists to explain things in a way that is easy for laypeople to understand. The media tends to seek out people who present powerful messages in a short time. However, the viewing public that receives these messages should ask whether those scientists' statements are backed by evidence and press for explanations until they are convinced.

Unfortunately, unless they choose to pursue university-preparatory programs in the sciences, high-school students in Japan have few opportunities to obtain basic science knowledge. I feel that, at the very least, introductory courses in physics, chemistry, and biology should be mandatory for all high-school students. These three subjects, especially biology, are particularly important for learning about organisms—in other words, for learning about the self. Students should learn the principles that constitute humankind as a basis of common knowledge. If this foundation were in place, perhaps everyone would be able to gauge whether information is accurate and act accordingly.

Preparing a Research Environment for the Next Generation

In April 2020, the Kyoto University Graduate School of Medicine established the Center for Cancer Immunotherapy and Immunobiology (CCII) and appointed me its first-ever director. The CCII is a comprehensive research facility where immunology (principles) and immunotherapy (clinical application) are investigated under one roof. Through close communication, researchers at the CCII can solve problems related to principles and clinical application and make progress in both. I would like to make the CCII a place for brilliant minds to gather from all over the world so that the organization can deliver an international message. In January 2021, the CCII will welcome Dr. Sidonia Fagarasan from Romania as its first professor. To not only attract but also retain those brilliant minds, the CCII uses English as a common language—not only for conversation but also for written documents and meeting minutes. One reason behind the establishment of the CCII was that although immunotherapy, which started in earnest in 2014, was born in Japan, the country where it is currently used the most frequently is the United States. I want to do whatever I can to help Japan take back the lead. Although it will be 2023 before construction of the CCII building is complete, research has already begun, and new staff members are being selected.

From the 1990s to the 2000s, several members of the Japanese Diet, led by the late Kato Koichi, formed a group that not only understood but actively championed science and technology. Thanks to their generous support, my generation of scientists made great strides in our research. However, supportive Diet members like Kato Koichi's group have nearly disappeared. For the generation of researchers in their fifties, who should be leading the world, these are dark days.

To remedy this sorry situation, I am working hard to build a framework that will give the young scientists of tomorrow access to the funds and opportunities to conduct research. In life science in particular, you never know unless you try. The important thing is to sow lots of seeds and make them grow. Governmental budgeting and public donations should be increased and used to support a wide variety of research projects. If the research support goes toward too narrow a target, the results of the research cannot make their way back to society as practical benefits because, as I have said over and over, you never know what will succeed, and the success rate is low. Conversely, many politicians and economists nowadays need to realize that life science has enormous economic effects. As I mention in Chapter 4, there is a reason the United States invests so heavily in life science—developments in life science lead to technological innovation. For example, unraveling the principles of light energy in photosynthesis would enable the application of vast quantities of solar energy in people's lives and industries of all kinds.

To Younger Generations

Many people seem to think of research as a distant world. Researchers need to have passion, a sense of wonder, and curiosity. Whatever they are researching, they should forge ahead with it if they have the impulse to know things, phenomena that inspire them, and the desire to discover and foster something. Research is just like listening to a stirring piece of music and feeling the urge to compose something stirring yourself. Of course, the levels and types of joy that people experience through music are as countless as the listeners themselves. The people who should be researchers are those who wonder whether a certain phenomenon is real, marvel at it, and want to know more about it.

At some point in their careers, medical students have to decide whether to become physicians or researchers. In my case, I was curious about intractable diseases that existing medicine could not cure. Why couldn't they be cured? Is there really no cure? Driven by the impulse to find out, I chose to become a researcher. Cases like mine, in which unraveling the principles of immunity led to the development of a new cancer therapy, occur only once every few decades. All I can say is that I have been blessed with incredibly good fortune.

Life is finite. Extending people's lifespans is not the objective of medical science. The mission of physicians is to help people live to their appointed times. I am already 78 years old. I have lived three quarters of my lifespan. I feel that my generation's greatest responsibility is to prepare an environment in which young people will want to accomplish something in a given field and work hard toward their goals. The current environment in Japan makes it incredibly difficult for the next generation to attempt to accomplish anything. Even with research at universities, other, non-research tasks consume massive amounts of time. I hope to create an environment where many researchers in many different fields can devote themselves to their research without distractions.

One of my teachers, Nishizuka Yasutomi, a former President of Kobe University, once told me something I will never forget: "Tasuku, the research environment in Japan is like a telephone pole in an open field. It needs to be like the rippling, many-ridged peaks of the Yatsugatake Mountains." In other words, we must create an environment that helps young people grow so that they can lead the world.

I particularly want people of younger generations to think about how they want to live out their one and only life and what they want to do with it. Everyone has a different definition of happiness. Happiness comes in all shapes and sizes. I think it is happier to arrive at the end of your life with the feeling that you have accomplished something than to die with regrets.

Acknowledgements

I express my overwhelming gratitude to the Cabinet Office of the Japanese government, whose generosity has enabled the publication of my book *Gan Men'ekiryoho towa Nani ka* [What is Cancer Immunotherapy?] in English *as Advances in Cancer Immunotherapy: From Serendipity to Cure.*

I also thank the following people for their tremendous cooperation: Andrew Gonzalez, Mutlow Hisako, Amy LB Frazier, and Tom Kain for their hard work on the translation itself and Dr. Ishida Yasumasa (Nara Institute of Science and Technology) and Dr. Agata Yasutoshi (Shiga University of Medical Science) for checking the content during the translation process and ensuring that the scientific terminology is accurate.

Lastly, I extend my thanks to Teshima Aki (Japan Publishing Industry Foundation for Culture [JPIC]) for her courteous correspondence and coordination throughout the translation of the book.

Honjo Tasuku

INTRODUCTION

For me, the joy of research is picking up a theme that most people have summarily dismissed as an ordinary rock, polishing that rock over a long period of time, and showing everyone that it was actually a diamond all along. If the value of a theme is already obvious, its value cannot increase any further. Themes of unknown value taken from a chaotic state are the ones with hidden, unforeseen potential to shine.

Whether the research theme one chooses will remain a rock or transform into a diamond is a matter of luck. The only way to unlock the future is to be brave and take on the unknown. Looking back, I have been blessed with good fortune on many occasions. All of that serendipity has made me realize that good fortune emerges from the dogged, day-by-day accumulation of little steps. Although hard work is not always rewarded, good fortune does not come to those who do not keep working resolutely toward their goals. Persistent hard work fosters a unique sensibility that can detect where something is hidden—an absolutely indispensable asset for biomedical science researchers. This sensibility also sometimes brings good fortune.

For researchers to be resolute and independent, I believe that they need the "six Cs": curiosity, challenge, courage, confidence, concentration, and continuation. First, a researcher must prize their own curiosity. Next, they need the courage to challenge the object of their curiosity. To do so, what a researcher needs most is complete confidence. A researcher must also concentrate on their research and continue it. However, all of this is easier said than done. Although the six Cs are rather difficult to pursue, I believe that if a researcher constantly works at them and strives to make progress day by day, a path will surely open for them.

The thrill of research is like finding a spring among overlooked rocks, building up that trickle of water into a stream, and then making it into a mighty river. In this book, as I reflect on my life as a researcher, I introduce cancer immunotherapy based on antibodies against PD-1, which my research group discovered. I also discuss a wide range of topics including the marvels of biological phenomena, the thrill of life science's exploration of the unknown, the nature of life itself, and the future of Japanese healthcare.

The Marvel of Immunity

General Rules of Biological Systems

DNA, the "blueprint of life," determines the amino-acid sequences and consequently the structures of proteins according to triplets of the four bases adenine (A), guanine (G), cytosine (C), and thymine (T). Using this code, DNA stores all the information for the roughly 20,000 proteins in the human body. The genetic information encoding a single protein is known as a gene. The genetic information conveyed through DNA determines the structure of a protein, which in turn determines that protein's function. This flow of information from DNA to protein—which occurs in all organisms on earth—is the central dogma of biology.

The smallest unit of life that possesses a complete copy of genetic information is the cell. The genetic information in DNA is basically identical across all the cells of an organism and is passed to daughter cells as they divide. Single-celled species self-reproduce through cell division. In contrast, multicellular species produce gametes to create descendants through fertilization, during which genetic information from two different individuals mixes together. Although single-celled species vastly outnumber multicellular organisms, the process of fertilization is considered to have played a major role in evolution.

Humans are an example of a multicellular organism that reproduces through fertilization. In our species, the genetic information in DNA is passed—largely unchanged—from parents to their children and their descendants. However, because both the mother and the father contribute genetic information to a fertilized egg, it is impossible for their child to have exactly the same set of genes as either one parent or the other. In addition, genetic makeup (genotype) differs among siblings because individual maternal and paternal gametes acquire different combinations of genes as they are produced.

If the genetic information in organisms never changed, life would never have evolved—the first-ever life form would have forever remained as initially fashioned. Over the eons, however, genetic information has been (and continues to be) altered: both gradually through small-scale changes (affecting single genes) and—on rare occasions—rapidly through large-scale (multigene) mutation. Darwinian thought holds that the results of these mutations are selected by the environment, leading to the evolution of organisms. Although impossible to prove, the theory of Darwinism is supported by various phenomena observed throughout the history of evolution.

Multicellular species include organisms as large as blue whales and as small as (and smaller than) jellyfish. Regardless of the size of an organism, each of the organism's cells contains various subcellular organelles that differ in function. For example, the nucleus of a cell stores genetic information; mitochondria produce energy; and the endoplasmic reticulum facilitates the secretion and processing of proteins. Furthermore, these diverse species all comprise multiple types of cells, each with its specific role in supporting the life of the organism to which it belongs. That type of diversity is a vital characteristic of multicellular organisms.

Characteristics of Multicellular Organisms

Coordinating the various cell types that compose multicellular organisms requires multiple high-level regulatory mechanisms. In other words, compared with single-celled species, multicellular organisms are complex, diverse, and flexible.

Complexity is relevant to the survival of organisms and species. For any organism, the ability to adapt to changes in its environment is crucial. Engineering has given us the word "robustness," a machine's capacity to withstand minor damage and continue to function. Organisms are equipped with a variety of mechanisms that enable them to survive dramatic environmental changes—a level of robustness that simple single- or double-layer regulatory systems would fail to ensure. Consequently, these species require complexity and diversity in their regulatory systems. Conversely, pinpoint accuracy and a lack of flexibility make machines more fragile. In the same way, regulatory mechanisms that are somewhat imprecise and "sloppy" enable multicellular organisms to deftly temper the effects of minor abnormalities and environmental changes.

If all the members of a given species—any species—had the same genotype, any shift in the environment would endanger the survival of not just a single organism but the species as a whole. Genotypic diversity enables a species to cope with environmental changes more successfully. The immune system is a prime example of the importance of diversity to life.

How Immunity Works

Broadly defined, immune cells comprise one of the functionally specialized cell types in multicellular species. Immune cells include lymphocytes, macrophages, natural killer cells, neutrophils, and basophils as well as various subsets within each cell type. Whether migrating through the blood or residing within tissues, each immune cell population plays its particular role, all of which come together to compose an impressive defense system. Immunity is broadly divided into two types: innate immunity and acquired immunity.

Innate immunity is present in all organisms, but science has yet to delineate its roles and mechanisms in single-celled organisms. However, our understanding of the principles of innate immunity in multicellular species has progressed rapidly during the last 20 years or so. Research—first in insects and then in mice and humans—has revealed that these disparate species all share the same fundamental system of innate immunity.

The functioning of innate immunity depends on the presence of "pattern-recognition" receptors (PRRs). Although these receptors initially were thought to be expressed only on the outer cell membranes of immune cells, recent research has revealed the presence of intracellular PRRs as well. Regardless of their location, PRRs recognize and respond to characteristic structural patterns in biomolecules, including carbohydrates, lipids, and proteins; in particular, intracellular PRRs bind to the nucleic acid (DNA and RNA) of infecting foreign microbes. For example, such a receptor may recognize the structure of a bacterial lipopolysaccharide and then alert other cells to the presence of harmful microbes or other foreign material. Consequently, these other cells—particularly macrophages—secrete cytokines (signaling molecules), which then stimulate various immune cells to phagocytose (engulf and destroy) offending microbes and inform the acquired immune system (described later) of the threat to the host organism.

Unlike the universality of innate immunity, acquired immunity—through which an organism's immune system "remembers" previous infections—has emerged only since the evolution of vertebrates. Acquired immunity is characterized by the presence of specialized immune cells called lymphocytes. Because each lymphocyte has its own, unique type of receptor, individual lymphocytes are able to recognize the nature of invaders of the host organism down to their smallest detail. The differences between these receptors enable an organism's immune system to identify and protect against almost as many types of foreign substances as there are lymphocytes.

Principles of Acquired Immunity

How, then, is acquired immunity capable of recognizing differences between invaders in such a sophisticated manner? The field of life science wrestled with this question for much of the twentieth century.

One of the pillars of acquired immunity is the production of antibodies (proteins that are produced by the immune system and that react with biomolecular "fingerprints" known as antigens). Early vaccines were developed based on empirical knowledge that the immune response following repeated exposure to a particular antigen (derived from a harmful microbe) is more powerful than the one after an organism's initial exposure. Broadly speaking, vaccination involves administering an antigen from a pathogen or foreign substance to an organism before that animal (or person) has developed the disease associated with the pathogen. In other words, vaccination primes an organism's immune system so that it responds vigorously to invading pathogens. In particular, vaccination results in the production of antibodies, which were first observed in the blood of animals by Emil von Behring and Kitasato Shibasaburo near the end of the nineteenth century.

Later, researchers were astonished to find that the antibodies animals and humans produced after immunization were always specific to the antigens they received. This finding arose from efforts to answer the question of how we, despite having a finite number of genes, are able to produce antibodies that bind so powerfully (highly specifically) to apparently countless foreign antigens.

The decisive answer to this question proved to be the phenomenon of V(D)J recombination, which Tonegawa Susumu and his colleagues discovered in 1977. These researchers found that during the differentiation of lymphocytes—unlike in any other cell types—various portions of antibody genes (the V, D, and J segments) are rearranged in different combinations in each lymphocyte. Previously, genes were considered to be nearly inviolable blueprints for the proteins they encoded. However, the discovery of V(D)J recombination showed that—at least in lymphocytes—the blocks of information in antibody genes can be rearranged as needed and in an unrestricted fashion.

Furthermore, in 2000, my laboratory discovered that the gene AID is responsible for a vaccine's ability to induce antibody memory. Specifically, we learned that the enzymes RAG-1 and RAG-2 accomplish the gene rearrangement that occurs during the process of lymphocyte differentiation discovered by Tonegawa and colleagues. We also learned that when a mature lymphocyte encounters the cognate antigen (the one that the lymphocyte recognizes), AID triggers the two additional processes of gene rearrangement called "somatic hypermutation" and "class switch recombination."

Somatic hypermutation enhances an antibody's ability to recognize and strongly bind an antigen, introducing near-random point mutations (substitutions of a single-base A, G, C, or T) in the DNA sequence of an antibody's antigen-binding site. Then, from among the many lymphocytes carrying antibody genes with those mutations, cells that produce antibodies with even greater binding affinity for the relevant antigen are selected.

Class switching is the mechanism that changes the type (class) of an antibody. Separate from its antigen-recognition site, every antibody has a key element that determines how it works. Class switching supplies the various functional types of antibodies, including IgA antibodies, which are secreted from mucus membranes to prevent the entry of invaders through that route, and IgG antibodies, which—together with complement proteins in the blood—prey on foreign microbes. Again, through the gene rearrangement processes, lymphocytes that express antibodies with high antigen-binding affinity are chosen for proliferation. This selection and enhanced proliferation of lymphocytes explains how the antibody "memory" against antigens persists in our body and how vaccines exert their effects.

Although somatic hypermutation and class switch recombination are completely different processes, the same molecule—AID—governs both. Consequently, AID engraves antigenic memories into the genes of lymphocytes. To reiterate, somatic diversification (which includes VDJ recombination) and subsequent selection, which are key to acquired immunity, occur only in lymphocytes. Furthermore, acquired immunity gets at the heart of life science by serving as a splendid illustration of Darwinian natural selection—the fundamental principle of biological evolution—within an individual. So how did acquired immunity evolve?

Subsequent research found that lampreys and hagfish, cyclostomes believed to be the oldest vertebrate species, already carry genetic mutations relevant to acquired immunity. Max Cooper (a 2018 Japan Prize laureate) and his colleagues discovered that the gene responsible for rearranging antibody genes in lampreys is, in fact, an ancestral form of AID. In addition, this type of somatic gene rearrangement was reported to occur in two classes of immune cells: B cells (B lymphocytes), which produce antibodies, and T cells (T lymphocytes), which facilitate antibody production or directly kill infected cells.

Evolutionarily speaking, RAG-1 and RAG-2, which direct the gene rearrangement that occurs during B-cell differentiation, suddenly arose just as fish species emerged. The structures and functions of RAG-1 and RAG-2 suggest that they were introduced as new genes through viral infection. If correct, this implies a truly amazing evolutionary process in which an abrupt viral infection of an organism's gametes caused genes to be divided and then rejoined in a different combination during an individual's developmental process. Unfortunately, there is no way to replicate these experiments of evolution, but we certainly have enough information to surmise the wonders of the evolution of life.

In both B and T cells, the advent of RAG-1 and RAG-2 replaced gene rearrangement during an organism's developmental stages with a mechanism of diversification, whose power rests in the large number of combinations in which gene fragments can be linked together. The ancestral form of AID lost its role here. In modern species, AID has assumed the role of generating antibodies with tremendously enhanced binding affinity in an antigen-specific manner (what makes vaccines successful) and by fine-tuning antibody specificity through the introduction of point mutations.

As described earlier, in contrast to innate immunity's hazy recognition of foreign microbes and materials, acquired immunity keenly discriminates among even the most minute characteristics of its targets. In this regard, acquired immunity is generally considered to be highly specific. That leads to another question: if the broad variety of these highly specific antibodies were to arise nearly randomly due to genetic mutation, would the resulting immunity successfully differentiate external enemies (that is, non-self) from the organism's own molecules, cells, and tissues (that is, self)?

A critical feature of immune systems is how they distinguish between self and non-self—a central question of immunology research for decades. In the 1950s, Frank Burnet insightfully proposed that the immunologic distinction between the host organism and foreign material is accomplished through the selection of clones (lineages of cells with exactly the same genes). He hypothesized that among the lymphocytes resulting from numerous genetic mutations and with their consequent various specificities, those that react to the organism's own antigens are destroyed. In contrast, only those lymphocytes that do not react against self components are allowed to survive.

Burnet's prediction hit the mark beautifully. In particular, it was discovered that T cells that react with an organism's own antigens die in the thymus during the process of differentiation from bone marrow-derived progenitors; they never mature or emerge in the blood again. Fully understanding this mechanism requires much more study. In contrast to T cells, B cells do not undergo direct selection because they must coordinate with mature T cells (those that are selected to ignore self-antigens) to produce antibodies. Therefore, the assumption is that the immune system's ability to discriminate between self and non-self rests on the elimination of self-reactive T cells.

Specificity and Regulation

To summarize the discussion so far, the immune system is a mechanism that marries incredible diversity with tremendous specificity.

In its biological context, specificity refers to recognition via binding. Thus, high specificity means rigor in binding affinity and strength. However, excessive specificity would pose problems. Ideally, the immune system as a whole would cast a net in all directions to trap any and all invading pathogens. In addition, an ideal immune system would not react to the host organism's antigens. These desirable characteristics would be curtailed if the immune system were to rely solely on the structure of antigen-recognizing receptors to achieve appropriate specificity.

In the case of T-cell antigen receptors, for instance, the extent of the diversity due to the reassortment of gene fragments will never be known and can only be estimated. However, examining individual receptors reveals a broad distribution curve of targets, ranging from those that bind tightly to those that bind only weakly. In other words, as with antibodies, the specificity of T-cell receptors is high but not absolute—binding affinity is not an all-or-nothing matter. T-cell receptors are able to distinguish foreign substances with a certain range of flexibility.

But what would happen in animals or individuals with genetically limited diversity of antibodies or antigen receptors? In experiments aiming to answer this question, mice were genetically manipulated to yield mutant animals with fewer types of antigen receptors expressed on lymphocytes than in normal mice. (Each lymphocyte, incidentally, can express only a single type of antigen receptor.) Despite their limited immune diversity, the genetically manipulated mice demonstrated nearly the same level of immune response as normal mice—a finding that emphasizes that neither antigen recognition nor receptor binding affinity is absolute. Instead, the experimental results suggest the presence of a mechanism through which information regarding receptor binding is transmitted inside the lymphocyte, such that the regulation of the signal modulates the level of antigen recognition.

In reality, lymphocyte function involves more than just antigen binding. Rather, relaying the "antigen bound" signal into the lymphocyte induces the phosphorylation of many intracellular molecules. This intracellular signal transduction system must induce gene expression, lymphocyte proliferation, and subsequent mobilization of other immune cells before the initiation of a fully competent immune response. Therefore, regulation of the relative threshold of signaling after antigen recognition is critical for an appropriate, effective immune response.

Currently, regulation of this threshold is known to involve molecules that act as "brakes" (such as CTLA-4 and PD-1) and as "accelerators" (for example, CD28 and ICOS). In addition, these molecular accelerators and brakes have been the targets of synthetic modulators of immune responses. Despite years of effort, none of the attempts to manipulate immune accelerators advantageously has been successful. However, the release of this immune brake is currently being used to advance the development of cancer immunotherapy, which offers a novel prospect for conquering this class of disease (see Chapter 2). Today, the most promising means of immune system regulation involve weakening the brake.

Overall Regulation of Immunity

The immune system is home to a myriad of cells, from lymphocytes and macrophages to neutrophils, basophils, and eosinophils. These cells circulate throughout an organism and—along with tissue-specific immune-related cells such as Langerhans cells in the skin and microglia in the brain—monitor every niche. In addition, these cell groups use biomolecular transmitters called chemokines and cytokines to communicate with each other, much like neurons convey messages by using intercellular transmitters. In the context of the immune system, chemokines direct cells regarding which way to move, whereas cytokines transmit signals regarding activation and inhibition from one cell to surrounding cells.

When stimulated by antigens, lymphocytes proliferate at blinding speed. Given that E. coli divides in as little as 20 minutes, the eight hours needed for T cells to divide may not seem to be particularly rapid at first glance. However, an E. coli cell has an approximate diameter of 1 μm, whereas the diameter of a lymphocyte is roughly 10 μm. In terms of volume, then, a lymphocyte is 1000 times larger than E. coli. If it divided at the same rate as E. coli, a lymphocyte would require roughly 330 hours to complete the process. The ability of lymphocytes to divide in only eight hours shows how efficiently they generate energy and synthesize proteins and also nucleic acids. But how do lymphocytes safely compress the 330 hours of activity into a mere eight hours? One has to wonder—but no one has ever experimentally addressed the mystery of the many-fold increase in efficiency. In fact, this practically abnormal proliferation of lymphocytes is known to cause major—albeit temporary—fluctuations in blood metabolites.

In mice, using anti-PD-1 antibodies to inhibit the immune brake resulted in rapid proliferation of lymphocytes, triggering behavioral abnormalities. To support the metabolic demand resulting from this rapid proliferation, the immune system consumes vast quantities of tryptophan and tyrosine, key precursors of neurotransmitters, thereby likely reducing the level of neurotransmitters in the blood. The same phenomenon occurs in humans: according to some recent studies, cancer immunotherapy comprising continuous administration of anti-PD-1 antibodies led to anxiety in some patients. These reports demonstrate a direct relationship between the immune system and the control of brain function through metabolism.

Interactions between the brain and the immune system have long been known. For example, steroid hormone therapy leads to a stress-mediated reduction in immune system activity. In another example, the nerve endings distributed throughout the intestine are connected to the intestinal immune system. Recent research suggests that Alzheimer disease may arise in part due to insufficient removal of immune waste products. Finally, immune cells are known to accumulate fat, thus forming atheromas (atheromatous plaques) and triggering atherosclerosis.

The immune system monitors regulatory systems throughout an organism and integrates their function. Excessive immune system activity, manifested as inflammatory responses, affects all of an organism's organs. Conversely, a weakened immune system can trigger the onset of cancer, systemic metabolic imbalance, obesity, and infection.

Particularly important is the finding that the immune system is intricately intertwined with aging. Specifically, T cells mature in the thymus, which gradually involutes (decreases in size) in adults; once adults reach their forties or so, the production of new T cells stops almost completely. How, then, can the body maintain sufficient lymphocytes despite this halt in T-cell production? The general belief is that the number of T cells remains constant because so-called "memory T cells" are long-lived and divide slowly due to weak stimulation by autoantigens (antigens from the organism itself). For these reasons, activating immune responses in elderly people through periodic vaccination is considered a promising means to slow the aging of the immune system.

Joining the extant nervous, metabolic, circulatory, and various regulatory systems, the immune system—particularly the acquired immune system—arose as vertebrates emerged in evolution. The immune system has the crucial role of coordinating these various systems, as it regulates both the overall internal environment of an organism as well as local niches in tissues.

Curing Cancer
with Anti-PD-1 Antibodies

Cancer Immunotherapy: The Birth of a Revolutionary Treatment

The Fight against Cancer

Cancer has long been considered the most difficult disease to conquer. Regardless of the cell type affected—whether skin, blood, bone, or otherwise—cancers result from the development of abnormal cells that evade the body's checkpoints to proliferate uncontrollably within and subsequently destroy normal tissue. Since 1981, cancer has been the leading cause of death in Japan. Simply not wanting to die of cancer is a powerful, common feeling.

Even compared with other fields of medical research, research on cancer therapy has received vast sums of funding and has occupied many researchers. For example, during the Nixon administration (1969–74), the United States government began waging a "War on Cancer." The legislation that launched this effort came on the heels of the Apollo program, which ultimately put humans on the moon.

The War on Cancer received considerable financial investment from the federal budget. Years later, the achievements of the project were reviewed. In short, the review concluded that although the project had deepened our understanding of cancer itself, it had yielded little regarding new ways to treat cancer. Efforts to find new cancer treatments have focused primarily on the development of new chemotherapeutic agents (chemical compounds). In fact, aside from the landmark development of the novel leukemia drug imatinib (approved in 2001 for use in the United States), research on chemotherapeutic agents during the last 30 years or so has yielded few results that represent dramatically new options—just new "flavors" of currently available drugs.

The general principle behind chemotherapeutic drugs is that they bind to a specific cellular molecule to inhibit its function and suppress cancer cell proliferation. Different chemotherapeutic agents work in different ways, on different types of molecules with different functions; some chemotherapeutics work better than others. Depending on how the drug works, the cancer could diminish in three months, six months, or sometimes one year. However, almost every time a cancer is treated with chemotherapeutic agents, the cancer metastasizes (establishes itself in another part of the body) and regrows. One explanation for this major ongoing problem is the cancer stem cell hypothesis. Although the question of whether cancer stem cells even exist is still under debate, the inability to completely cure cancer by using chemical compounds strongly supports the hypothesis. Although some individual chemotherapeutic agents are rather effective, it seems to me that the cancer stem cell hypothesis emerged from the inability to cure cancer through chemical means.

A New Avenue of Cancer Treatment

Conventionally, surgical resection, radiation therapy, and chemotherapy are considered the mainstays of cancer treatment. All three of these modalities focus mechanistically on attacking cancer cells from outside the body: by physically removing cancerous tissue (surgical resection) or by using exogenous agents (radiation and chemicals [drugs]) to kill cancerous cells. The problem with all of these methods is that they are relatively nonselective: they do not differentiate very well between healthy cells and abnormal cancer cells. Consequently, these traditional modes of cancer treatment are fraught with adverse side effects.

However, a completely different concept of cancer treatment—the idea of harnessing the body's own immune system to cure cancer—has been around for over 100 years. This concept was first advanced by the American physician William Coley, who reported that he was actually able to cure patients' cancers after administering bacterial toxins to stimulate their immune systems. Frank Burnet, whom some call the "father of modern immunology," also believed that "training" the immune system to treat cancer (implementing cancer immunotherapy) was theoretically possible. Although many researchers later attempted various forms of cancer immunotherapy to varying degrees of success, none of the attempts completely succeeded in the end. Before going into the history of immunotherapy, however, I want to summarize the basic concepts of cancer immunotherapy.

Immunologists hold that cancer cells were once normal cells in the body but became different for some reason or another (in many cases, genetic mutation). Cancer cells express so-called "neoantigens" (new or different cell markers). All normal cells are "self," whereas cancer cells are "non-self" due to the expression of neoantigens. Therefore, the immune system has latent potential to distinguish cancer cells from the body's own cells and subsequently to destroy cancer cells. The immune system's ability to differentiate normal (self) cells from cancerous (non-self) ones is the phenomenon known as "immune surveillance." However, the markedly increased proliferative ability of cancer cells upsets the balance of power between immune cells and cancer cells, ultimately overwhelming the immune system. Consequently, cancer cells keep growing and spreading: immune surveillance has broken down.

The overexuberant proliferation of cancer cells disrupts the immune system and causes the body to lapse into a persistent state of "immune tolerance," where it no longer responds to or removes cancer cells. For many years, no one could determine whether this lapse into immune tolerance actually happened.

Activating Immunity by Releasing the "Brake"

To apply automotive terms to cancer immunotherapy, the immune system could be reactivated in two ways: by stepping on the "accelerator" or by releasing (or destroying) the "brake." Most conventional cancer treatments attempt to reenergize cancer-suppressed immune systems by stepping harder on the "accelerator." However, researchers eventually realized that the problem is not with the immune system's accelerator. Instead, immune tolerance occurs because the brake is pressed all the way down, such that releasing the brake is crucial to reactivating immune surveillance to recognize and eradicate "non-self" cancer cells. This discovery paved the way for anti-PD-1 antibody therapy.

The discovery and understanding of the immune brake came relatively late. CTLA-4 (a protein in T cells that helps down-regulate immune responses) was discovered in 1987, and my laboratory discovered PD-1 in 1992. From

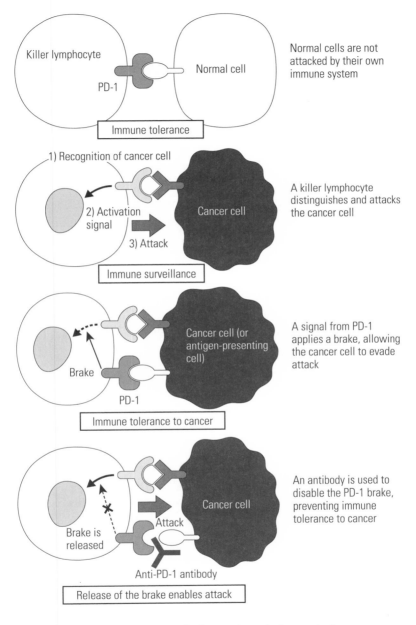

Killer lymphocyte

PD-1

Normal cell

Normal cells are not attacked by their own immune system

Immune tolerance

1) Recognition of cancer cell

2) Activation signal

3) Attack

Cancer cell

A killer lymphocyte distinguishes and attacks the cancer cell

Immune surveillance

Cancer cell (or antigen-presenting cell)

Brake

PD-1

A signal from PD-1 applies a brake, allowing the cancer cell to evade attack

Immune tolerance to cancer

Brake is released

Attack

Cancer cell

An antibody is used to disable the PD-1 brake, preventing immune tolerance to cancer

Anti-PD-1 antibody

Release of the brake enables attack

Figure 1. Using PD-1 antibodies to release the immune brake

the structure of PD-1, we began to suspect that it might act as an immune brake in 1995. By studying PD-1 knockout mice (mice lacking PD-1), we were able to prove that PD-1 is indeed an immune brake. Using anti-PD-1 antibodies to destroy the PD-1 immune brake reenergizes the immune system, once again enabling it to target and attack cancer cells (Figure 1).

The Unrelenting Pursuit of Ever-Changing Cancer

Cancer cells accumulate gene mutations 100 to 1000 times more frequently than normal cells do. Consequently, the non-self antigens expressed by cancer cells do not stay constant but rather change with an alarming frequency. Therefore, immunotherapy that targets only a single type of neoantigen would yield the same poor results as chemotherapy and would be rendered completely ineffective if cancer cells with new neoantigens were to arise.

In contrast, destroying the immune brake can mobilize all lymphocytes in the immune system, particularly killer lymphocytes (cytotoxic T cells, which possess the ability to destroy cancer cells). The key here is that T-cell receptors, the recognition molecules of lymphocytes, have nearly infinite diversity, a result of lymphocytes actively rearranging their own T-cell receptor genes. The resulting diversity of recognition is a major distinguishing characteristic of immunity. Thanks to this diversity, no matter how much cancer cells change, immune cells can pursue cancer cell mutations to any extent.

Like their counterparts that confer protection against pathogens, cancer vaccines, a conventional form of cancer immunotherapy, were designed to enhance the immune system by focusing on a specific antigen. In contrast, disengaging the immune brake by using the anti-PD-1 antibody is not restricted to the immune reaction against a particular antigen; it gives the immune system the power to pursue and eliminate cancer cells regardless of their antigenic identity.

This result has been applied in clinical practice. Currently, as Table 1 shows, anti-PD-1 (or PD-L1) antibodies have been approved and are covered by national health insurance in Japan for various cancers. More than 1000 clinical trials are currently in progress around the world. I believe that the day will soon come when the PD-1 (or PD-L1)-blocking therapy is applied to nearly all types of cancer.

Table 1. Anti-PD-1 and PD-L1 antibodies approved for clinical use in Japan (as of January 2019)

PRODUCT	INDICATIONS
Anti-PD-1 antibody	
Nivolumab	Melanoma, non-small-cell lung cancer, renal-cell cancer, Hodgkin lymphoma, head and neck cancer, stomach cancer, malignant pleural mesothelioma
Pembrolizumab	Melanoma, non-small-cell lung cancer, Hodgkin lymphoma, urothelial carcinoma, microsatellite instability-high (MSI-High) solid tumors
Anti-PD-L1 antibody	
Avelumab	Merkel cell carcinoma
Atezolizumab	Non-small-cell lung cancer
Durvalumab	Non-small-cell lung cancer

Key Differences between Immunotherapy and Conventional Therapy

Immunotherapy offers three main advantages over conventional anticancer therapeutic modalities (chemotherapy, radiation therapy, and surgery). The first is versatility. Whereas chemotherapeutic agents work on only specific types of cancer depending on the particular drug, anti-PD-1 antibodies can work on all cancers, even if their effectiveness (efficacy) might differ somewhat between disease types. Second, as the cases presented later will illustrate, once anti-PD-1 antibodies begin to work, the therapeutic effect lasts for several years—even if the medication is discontinued in three to six months. Again, this benefit of anti-PD-1 antibodies differs from conventional chemotherapeutics, which often start to wane in efficacy even during the course of treatment. Third, anti-PD-1 antibodies cause markedly fewer side effects than conventional anticancer agents. Conversely, well-known and common side effects of chemotherapeutics include nausea, vomiting, and hair loss. However, anti-PD-1 antibody treatment is not completely without side effects—autoimmune diseases, which result from enhancement of the immune system, could develop (however infrequently) in various organs. Thorough follow-up is necessary to monitor this potential problem in patients.

Astonishing Therapeutic Outcomes

Clinical research on anti-PD-1 antibodies began in 2006 in the United States and 2009 in Japan. At that time, few physicians believed that immunotherapy would be effective against cancer. Securing governmental approval for the use of a particular product—a medical device, drug, or other treatment—entails a process of "clinical trials," the first phase of which serves to answer the question of whether the target product is safe. For anti-PD-1 antibodies, these Phase I trials involved patients with various types of cancers (lung cancer, melanoma, and kidney [renal-cell] cancer, for example), many of whom were in very advanced stages of their disease and had little time left to live (Table 2). However, not only was anti-PD-1 antibody treatment safe, a surprising large percentage of the patients—18% to 28%—responded favorably to the treatment. In addition, many patients survived for 12 months or longer as their tumors either shrank or remained the same size. These initial clinical studies began convincing skeptics that cancer immunotherapy and anti-PD-1 antibody treatments were not ill-conceived, unattainable therapeutic options.

Upon seeing these astounding therapeutic outcomes, pharmaceutical companies around the world began showing interest in anti-PD-1 antibodies. Several additional clinical studies and trials are now underway as well. Here at Kyoto University, for example, we have been collaborating with our

Table 2. Therapeutic outcomes achieved with anti-PD-1 antibodies

	No. of responders/ all patients	Response rate	No. of responders whose response lasted ≥12 months	Progression-free survival rate at 24 weeks
Melanoma	26/94	28%	≥2 years, 2; 12–23 months, 11	41%
Non-small-cell lung cancer	14/76	18%	≥2 years: 1; 12–23 months: 1 (of 18 patients recorded)	26%
Renal-cell cancer	9/33	27%	12–23 months, 5	56%

This table has been modified with permission from Topalian, S. L. et al. 2012. "Safety, Activity, and Immune Correlates of Anti-PD-1 Antibody in Cancer," Table 2. *New England Journal of Medicine* 366, 2443–2454.

Department of Gynecology and Obstetrics in a clinical trial for end-stage ovarian cancer. To date, 20% of participants have survived long-term (five years or more), a result comparable to other trials testing anti-PD-1 antibodies in other types of cancer. Patients who were told they had only a few months left to live have become completely healthy after undergoing anti-PD-1 immunotherapy, and, demonstrating their markedly improved quality of life, some of them have even returned to hobby activities, such as golfing.

Powerful, Long-Term Efficacy

One American clinical trial recruited roughly 400 patients with previously untreated melanoma (Figure 2). Half of the patients were assigned to receive anti-PD-1 antibody therapy. The remaining participants were to receive chemotherapy comprising dacarbazine, which was considered the most effective treatment for melanoma at that time. The trial was double-blind, meaning that neither the physicians nor the patients knew which therapy a participant received. The results of the trial were reported in 2014 and showed that slightly more than 70% of patients who received anti-PD-1 immunotherapy were still alive at 17 months after starting treatment. This figure is nearly identical to the survival rate achieved during the previous 6 months of the trial.

In contrast, among patients who received dacarbazine chemotherapy, the survival rate at 15 months was only around 20% and plummeted thereafter. At this point, the study results showed that the effectiveness of anti-PD-1 antibodies was considerably higher and longer-lasting than the conventional melanoma treatment regimen, and the trial was terminated early. The investigators deemed that it would be ethically unsuitable to continue the trial and continue to provide numerous patients with the inferior conventional treatment. Currently, anti-PD-1 antibodies are covered by health insurance in Japan for the treatment of melanoma.

The efficacy of anti-PD-1 antibodies varies somewhat between types of cancer. Sometimes anti-PD-1 antibodies work even better than they do for ovarian cancer and melanoma! In one study of Hodgkin lymphoma, a type of blood cancer, all 23 patients who received anti-PD-1 antibodies demonstrated at least a 20% reduction in tumor volume. Even better, in more than

Figure 2. Clinical trial results for melanoma

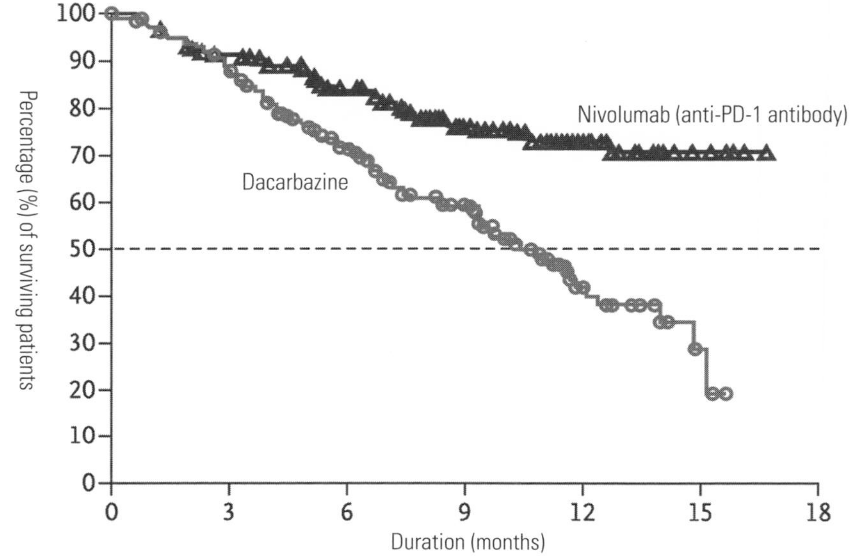

This figure has been modified with permission from Robert, C. et al. 2015. "Nivolumab in Previously Untreated Melanoma without BRAF Mutation," Figure 1A. *New England Journal of Medicine* 372, 320–330.

half of anti-PD-1-treated patients, the tumors shrank to less than half their original sizes. Anti-PD-1 antibodies worked extremely well for nearly all of these patients with Hodgkin lymphoma.

The Challenges of Increasing the Number of Responders and Identifying Responders in Advance

The current problem in anti-PD-1 immunotherapy—and cancer immuno-therapy in general—is that some patients respond to it whereas others respond very little. Although anti-PD-1 antibody therapy works well in almost all cases of Hodgkin lymphoma, similar levels of efficacy are likely only possible in certain types of cancer. Unfortunately, a proportion of patients with other types of cancer show a near total lack of response to anti-PD-1 antibodies.

Therefore, the next problem to tackle in the development of anti-PD-1 antibodies is how to make them work better in patients who respond poorly to them currently. To that end, various companies have combined anti-PD-1 antibodies with other therapies. Another issue is to identify some sort of indicator that distinguishes responders from non-responders before treatment begins. Such an indicator would be greatly helpful to patients, physicians, and insurers. These are two major issues currently facing the development of anti-PD-1 antibody therapy.

An Expanding Market

Given that the antitumor effect of anti-PD-1 antibodies defies conventional notions of what cancer therapy can achieve, almost all major pharmaceutical companies around the world have now started pursuing the research and development of anti-PD-1 antibodies.

In 2002, Ono Pharmaceutical Co., Ltd., and I jointly filed the first patent application for an anti-PD-1 antibody. This patent is now established worldwide. However, the American pharmaceutical company Merck and Co., Inc. has since begun to market their own anti-PD-1 antibody, sparking a fierce ongoing legal battle with Bristol Myers Squibb, which collaborated with Ono Pharmaceutical on anti-PD-1 research and development. Several other leading pharmaceutical companies, including Roche, AstraZeneca, and Pfizer, have also stepped into the anti-PD-1 antibody arena. In the next 10 years, anti-PD-1 antibodies are likely to become a first-line treatment for cancer, and the predicted market share for anti-PD-1 antibodies is on the order of tens of billions of dollars per year.

Advancements in Immunology and the History of Cancer Immunotherapy

The History of Immunotherapy

As I mentioned earlier, cancer immunotherapy dates back to the clinical experience of William Coley during the 1890s. Coley's experience showed him that cancer could be cured by using bacterial toxins to stimulate the body's immune system to recognize and eliminate cancerous cells. However, the treatment involved powerful side effects and lacked sufficient evidence of efficacy.

The concept of immunotherapy reemerged in the mid-twentieth century when Frank Burnet introduced the immune concepts of "self" and "non-self." These concepts gave rise to the idea that, in the process from changing from normal cells that express self antigens, cancerous tumors start producing new, non-self antigens (neoantigens). Burnet also advocated the theoretical application of immune surveillance in this context (elimination of non-self [cancer] by the immune system).

However, the subsequent history of immunotherapy has been anything but straightforward. Evidence that cancer could be controlled with immunity was only circumstantial, initially. In addition, as immunology research advanced, new molecules were discovered. However, despite numerous creative attempts, applying the immune system to anticancer treatment was not particularly successful. At the beginning of the 2000s, clinical experts viewed cancer immunotherapy with skepticism. In retrospect, this skepticism likely arose because everyone was thinking only of stepping on the immune system accelerator—and forgetting about the brake.

Circumstantial Evidence for the Involvement of the Immune System in Cancer

A great deal of circumstantial evidence has indicated that the likelihood of cancer increases or decreases depending on how well the immune system functions. For example, administering carcinogens to mice with defective immune systems (immunodeficient mice) increases their incidence of cancer compared with that in normal mice. In addition, long-term follow-up data have revealed that cancer develops more frequently in patients who receive immunosuppressants for organ transplantation than those that do not.

Conversely, some cases see therapeutic effects. During bone marrow transplantation for leukemia, donor lymphocytes are known to attack leukemic cells and thus offer the potential for a cure. In addition, some clinical cases of bone marrow transplantation have temporarily produced an extremely powerful immune response that cures other types of cancer.

These findings have led many to believe that immune surveillance is real and that cancer develops when immunity is weak.

The Concept of Immune Tolerance Is Born

One of the most important functions of the immune system is recognizing and attacking foreign enemies. To put it the other way around, the immune system does not attack its own body. Regardless of how prolifically or powerfully it could kill foreign enemies, the immune system would serve no purpose if it were to kill its own host organism. Immune tolerance is the mechanism that tells the immune system not to do so.

Immune tolerance is a fundamental concept involving the distinction between self and non-self and was advocated by Frank Burnet and Peter Medawar in the 1940s and 1950s. The researchers behind the idea proposed that lymphocytes that would recognize and attack cells carrying self antigens are selectively destroyed (clonal selection theory; here, "clone" refers to a line of cells) before they begin to circulate throughout the body. By destroying all lymphocytes reacting against self antigens, the immune system becomes tolerant to the self antigens that are expressed on normal, healthy cells in the body. A particularly attractive feature of this theory is its recapitulation of Darwinian selection within an organism. This compelling idea spurred incredible development in immunology and was confirmed to be fundamentally sound through subsequent research.

Thus, the concept of immune tolerance was constructed to explain how the immune system ignores (tolerates) cells that express self antigens. Conversely, the immune surveillance of cancer rests on an immune system that keenly discerns cells that were once self but are now—at least in part—nonself due to the expression of neoantigens.

Concurrent Developments in Immunology

In the late 1970s, the field of immunology grew by leaps and bounds. During this period, immunology was believed to be applicable to cancer treatment, a notion that spawned furious research on a variety of methods. One involved using cytokines (proteins secreted by immune cells) to activate the immune system. During the 1980s, several cytokines were discovered one after another. One family of cytokines was named "interleukins" (IL) because they were thought to support communication between ("inter-") blood cells (for example, leukocytes). The interleukins are numbered according to the order in which they were discovered. My laboratory colleagues and I discovered IL-4 and IL-5, and Kishimoto Tadamitsu discovered IL-6. To date, more than 30 interleukins have been identified.

As our overall grasp of immunity has progressed from a vague conceptualization to a molecular level-understanding, cancer immunotherapy has attempted to apply this growing base of knowledge toward activating the immune surveillance of cancer. These attempts led to the discovery of IL-2 and interferon gamma (IFN-γ). However, these agents produced severe side effects when administered directly to patients, causing this potential anticancer therapy to fall immediately out of favor.

One of these attempts was by Steven Rosenberg of the National Cancer Institute in the United States, who devised lymphokine-activated killer (LAK) therapy—a type of "adoptive immunotherapy." In adoptive immunotherapy, various immune cells are collected from a patient, grown and activated in the laboratory, and finally returned to the donor. In LAK therapy, lymphocytes are harvested from patients with cancer, stimulated with IL-2, and then reinfused into the patient. In an offshoot of adoptive immunotherapy, dendritic cells (which present antigens to lymphocytes and secrete cytokines) are engineered to recognize tumor antigens and activate lymphocytes before being returned to the body. In fact, Ralph Steinman—the scientist who discovered dendritic cells—used activated dendritic cells to treat his own cancer. However, none of the creative applications of adoptive immunotherapy to treating cancer accomplished any noteworthy clinical success.

Neoantigens and Vaccines

During the late 1980s and into the 1990s, Thierry Boon and others hypothesized that cancer involved the expression of specific non-self neoantigens. Boon's idea was that, at some point, immune tolerance would cease to ignore cells expressing tumor-specific neoantigens and that the immune system would appropriately monitor and eliminate cancerous cells. In addition, in the context of cancer, the immune system conceivably might switch between states of surveillance and tolerance. Boon and his colleagues actually managed to isolate neoantigens and prove their hypothesis, but the simple exploitation of neoantigens in an anticancer therapy was unsuccessful.

In current cancer vaccine therapy, tumor-specific antigens are used as vaccines to reactivate the immune system. Cancer vaccines initially sparked exorbitant funding and talk of commercialization. However, as Kitano Shigehisa stated in a column in the April 2016 issue of the journal *Kagaku* (Science), there was no real sense that cancer vaccines worked in clinical practice. Cancer vaccine success stories involving one or two cases cropped up occasionally, but cancers also have a certain probability of spontaneous remission. So, did the vaccine actually work in the sporadic cases of cure? The cause-and-effect relationship remains unclear.

Pessimism during the Early 2000s

The essential concept underlying all of these attempts was to activate the immune system to eliminate cancer. Methods for activating the immune system included combining various immune cells or vaccines (cancer-specific peptides) with systems outside or inside the body. However, the fundamental principles behind these different methods were the same.

Many versions of cancer immunotherapy underwent testing in clinical trials. However, approval proved hard to secure. In the United States, for example, cancer immunotherapy failed to receive approval from the Food and Drug Administration and was therefore unavailable for use by general clinicians. At various times, hopes for cancer immunotherapy were quite high; IFN-γ was lauded as a cure for cancer at the time of its discovery, for example. However, time and again, these hopes were dashed.

Therefore, clinical cancer specialists had grown weary of cancer immunotherapy by the turn of the millennium. For decades, immunologists had brought every possible therapeutic tool they could to clinical practice, claiming that this one or that one would work. However, even when the logic underlying these tools was sound, they all ultimately failed in clinical settings. Clinical cancer specialists grew more and more skeptical of cancer immunotherapy as a practical therapeutic option.

Consequently, when we wanted to tackle an early clinical trial using PD-1 in the early 2000s, no major pharmaceutical company would fund it. In their eyes, cancer immunotherapy had been dealt a fatal blow; the message was that we should move on already.

Research on the Role of T Cells

Here, the discussion merits another look at how immunity works and how that understanding has developed. In William Coley's day in the late nineteenth century, no one knew about T cells or B cells. During that same period, Kitasato Shibasaburo and Emil von Behring reported that factors capable of rendering pathogens harmless (what we know to be antibodies today) are produced in the blood. It was not until the 1960s that the distinctions between and roles of B and T cells started to become clear.

The "B" in "B cells" refers to the bursa of Fabricius, an anatomic feature of birds and where lymphocytes that produce antibodies were first found. In contrast, "T" lymphocytes ("T cells") are derived from the thymus. Researchers learned that the removal of the thymus inhibits the body's immune response, and lymphocytes specific to that response disappear. Later, proteins unique to each of these two types of lymphocytes were discovered, and the differential expression of these proteins was used to differentiate between T cells and B cells.

Our understanding of immune response regulation gradually evolved as well. One question involved the role of T cells in regard to antibody production by B cells. Efforts to answer this question revealed that T cells include populations of "helper T cells," which participate in immune regulation, and "killer (cytotoxic) T cells," which destroy non-self cells. Whereas the surfaces of helper T cells were found to contain CD4 molecules, killer cells carried CD8 molecules. The conclusion, then, was that T cells carrying CD8 molecules (CD8+ cells) were the killer cells that destroy cancer.

T Cells Regulate Immune Responses

What accomplishes immune tolerance? The initial answer was clonal selection. However, another concept later emerged: the idea that tolerance is about more than just selection—the regulation of immunity also plays a role. That is, immune tolerance involves a mechanism that recognizes antigens but suppresses the response to them.

This concept was first proposed by Richard Gershon in the 1970s, and Tada Tomio later constructed a model of this regulatory mechanism. According to Dr. Tada's model, CD8+ T cells suppressed immunity. However, because Dr. Tada also incorrectly hypothesized that this immune suppression was achieved through specific gene loci, the theory of suppressor T cells temporarily faded from the academic world. However, this suppressor role is now understood to be played by a population of T cells called "regulatory T cells" (Treg cells).

Knowledge of Tregs dates all the way back to 1969, when Nishizuka Yasuaki and Sakakura Teruyo at the Aichi Cancer Center discovered that removing the thymus of three-day-old mice triggered autoimmune symptoms. From there, Dr. Nishizuka and colleagues crafted a model in which autoimmune diseases developed when suppressor T cells could not be produced in the thymus. Later, cells expressing a protein called FOXP3, which was identified in humans, were found to be involved in the suppression of the immune response. The current understanding is that Treg cells that express both FOXP3 and CD4 (FOXP3+ CD4+ Tregs) suppress the immune response to self antigens.

However, the mechanism by which FOXP3+ T cells suppress immune responses has yet to be fully explained. FOXP3 is a transcription factor; in other words, it regulates the expression of various genes—that is, how much protein is produced from a particular gene at a particular time. As a transcription factor, FOXP3 does not work directly on proteins but instead functions within the cell nucleus to regulate the genes that lead to those proteins. We know that FOXP3 is important to the regulation of immune responses, but the mechanism through which it supervises gene expression remains unclear. Another intriguing finding is that FOXP3+ T cells coexpress both CTLA-4 (a protein involved in down-regulating immune responses) and PD-1 molecules (another down-regulator of immune reactions); clear consensus regarding this molecular-level mechanism has not yet been reached. And as has been the pattern, unfortunately, few of the many attempts to use Tregs clinically in anticancer therapy have succeeded.

Focusing on the Killer Cell Brake

How are CD8+ killer cells activated, then? Previous research focused on the regulation of activation: adding antigens into an experimental system, making the antigens recognizable, and increasing the number of lymphocytes to boost immune response. In the mid-1990s, immune system regulation was revealed to involve both positive and negative regulatory components. The first negative regulatory mechanism discovered involved the molecule CTLA-4. In this novel model, T-cell activation involved T-cell receptors and the positive regulatory molecule called CD28, whereas CTLA-4 acted as a brake to prevent overactivation.

Although immunologists believed that tumor immune surveillance existed, they kept hitting a wall when they applied their ideas to therapy. Despite hard work and copious knowledge, their efforts to transition from the research laboratory to the clinic bore little fruit. In hindsight, these struggles were likely due to the failure to realize that immune system activation is regulated not only by accelerators but also by brakes.

This realization came much later. Although CTLA-4 (an immune system brake) was discovered in 1987, its function was not understood until 1995. Immunologists generated mice that lacked the CTLA-4 gene (CTLA-4 knockout mice) and found that all of the mice developed serious autoimmune diseases and died before they reached five weeks of age. This study and various follow-up experiments enabled Dr. James P. Allison to report for the first time in 1996 that the antibody-mediated CTLA-4 blockade suppresses cancer.

In 1992, we discovered PD-1; by 1996, we had generated PD-1 knockout mice and confirmed at the laboratory level that PD-1 is a negative regulatory factor of immune activation. Around this same time, Dr. Allison's paper regarding CTLA-4 was published. Naturally, we also thought about the implications for anticancer therapy. Dr. Allison's findings showed that the antibody-mediated CTLA-4 blockade certainly activates tumor immune surveillance, but two papers published one year earlier (in 1995) indicated that the complete absence of CTLA-4 in knockout mice leads to the early death of all the gene-targeted mice due to severe autoimmune disease. Based on this finding, we believed the clinical application of the CTLA-4 blockade would be difficult because its side effects were too harsh. On the other hand, we have found that PD-1 gene knockout generates much milder symptoms (detailed in the next section).

The History of Anti-PD-1 Antibody Therapy Research and Development

A Serendipitous Discovery

We discovered PD-1 by pure chance in 1992 as we attempted to understand the mechanism underlying the selective cell death of self-reactive lymphocytes in the thymus. A graduate student in my laboratory, Ishida Yasumasa (currently at the Nara Institute of Science and Technology), elucidated the cDNA sequence of PD-1, which immediately revealed that the molecular structure of PD-1 was that of a membrane-bound receptor in lymphocytes. In addition, two tyrosine residues, which are considered necessary for transducing signals into cells, were preserved in the intracellular (cytoplasmic) region of PD-1. Although PD-1 was thus presumed to be a membrane receptor involved in lymphocyte signal transduction, we did not know specifically what it did.

Naturally, we wanted to figure out what PD-1 actually was. Our investigations showed that the molecule has unique structural properties and that it is expressed on very few types of cells—activated B cells and T cells, specifically, and not on almost any other cells. Therefore, we surmised that PD-1 may play a unique role in the immune system.

Similarities in Autoimmune Diseases between Humans and PD-1 Knockout Mice

At the time we discovered PD-1, we set out to prepare PD-1 gene knockout mice; this technique was still fairly new then. Handling the task was a dermatologist and graduate student in my laboratory, Nishimura Hiroyuki (currently with the Shiga Medical Center for Adults), who struggled mightily to get the desired results. Although the technical process of knocking out the PD-1 gene in mice went incredibly smoothly, taking only about one year, the mice showed no symptoms. Dr. Nishimura then consulted with Professor Minato Nagahiro (Kyoto University), an immunologist, who pointed out that mice sometimes need to be inbred in order for various forms of immune system dysregulation to emerge. Preparing inbred mice from the PD-1 knockout line required approximately 10 generations of backcrossing, a process that took about two years.

Finally, in the middle of 1996, we obtained mice that appeared to demonstrate an enhanced immune response. After detailed investigation, our first paper regarding the PD-1 knockout experiments was published in 1998, followed by another publication in 1999. The crucial point here is that the manifested symptoms depended on the pedigree of the knockout mouse. For example, black-strain mice developed autoimmune nephritis and arthritis, whereas white-strain mice developed autoimmune dilated cardiomyopathy. In addition, in mice that already demonstrated specific autoimmune symptoms, deletion of PD-1 markedly exacerbated those symptoms. For example, the black-strain PD-1 knockout mice began to show signs of nephritis and arthritis at three to six months of age and started dying at around one year. We believe this onset to be relatively gradual for autoimmune disease in mice and consider it comparable to the rate at which autoimmune diseases develop in humans.

How Is the Immune System Brake Transmitted into Cells?

Once we observed the structure of PD-1, we presumed that the two well-preserved tyrosine residues were involved in PD-1's function. The amino acid sequence surrounding these tyrosines resembled the immunoreceptor tyrosine-based activation motif (ITAM), a structural feature that was discovered in 1995 as an activation signal trigger. Just as we were thinking that PD-1 was a bit different from ITAMs, scholars were discovering and reporting on immunoreceptor tyrosine-based inhibition motifs (ITIMs), which are inhibitory signal-releasing tyrosines and their surrounding amino acid structures.

Using the new information regarding ITIMs, we created PD-1 sequences in which we mutated (changed) one or both of these tyrosines to other amino acids (thus modifying or destroying PD-1's ability to act as an immune system brake), expressed the mutants in B cells, and examined the transduction and mechanism of the inhibitory signals released by tyrosines. Of the two tyrosines, the downstream tyrosine is more important; when PD-1 receives a signal, the downstream tyrosine undergoes phosphorylation, and a phosphatase (SHP-2) binds to the phosphorylated tyrosine residue. Through incredibly elegant experiments, Okazaki Taku (currently at Tokushima University) discovered in 2001 that when SHP-2 acts on molecules that had been phosphorylated by lymphocyte activation signals, these molecules become dephosphorylated and consequently trigger changes in the overall amount of immune activation signals, depending on the molecule involved.

This discovery definitively proved at the molecular level that PD-1 acts as an immune brake and provided a foundation for proceeding confidently with subsequent research.

Binding Partner Molecules Are Expressed in Various Cells

Given that PD-1 has the structure of a cell-surface receptor, there must be a protein (ligand) that binds to it. However, this ligand was difficult to find despite meticulous searches. Around this time (1998), the Biacore device, which could electronically measure trace protein binding, was developed. I spoke with Steve Clark of Genetics Institute, an American venture laboratory that owned a Biacore, to set up a collaboration and sent him the requisite reagents and cells for development.

Because we had not yet published any papers about PD-1's function, the scientists at Genetics Institute knew practically nothing about PD-1. Luckily, however, Professor Gordon Freeman of Harvard University (Dana Farber Cancer Institute), who had been collaborating separately with Genetics Institute, had identified the cDNA of a series of proteins called the B7 family. In fact, PD-1 was a member of this large family. After thoroughly screening the entire B7 family, we found one member that turned out to be a ligand that binds to PD-1; this ligand is now known as "PD-L1." We published this finding in 2000.

PD-1 ligands are expressed on antigen-presenting cells. Antigen-presenting cells are macrophages and B cells that recognize antigens, incorporate them, and bind the antigenic peptides to the major histocompatibility complex (an antigen-presenting membrane molecule) so that antigens can be recognized by T cells. When an antigen is presented to a lymphocyte, the lymphocyte recognizes the antigen and binds to it; antigen binding thereby activates the lymphocyte. Remember, however, that PD-1 acts as an immune system brake: the PD-1 ligands on antigen-presenting cells step on the PD-1 brake to prevent excessive activation of T cells.

In an incredibly fascinating discovery, various cells besides antigen-presenting cells have been found to express PD-1 ligands. In particular, Dr. Freeman and colleagues learned that PD-1 ligands are expressed by various cancer cells. We and Dr. Freeman's group co-authored the paper that reported the discovery of PD-1 ligands.

Renewed Confidence in Cancer Immunotherapy

The above discoveries have made it clear that PD-1 is a negative immune regulatory factor. To summarize, PD-1 acts as an immune system brake. Destroying this brake by knocking out the PD-1 gene enhanced immune function, ultimately triggering autoimmune diseases in the mutant mice. In addition, the autoimmune symptoms in the PD-1 knockout mice were far milder and their onset more gradual than those in mice lacking a previously known immune regulator, CTLA-4. Unlike the mild autoimmunity of the PD-1 knockout mice, the CTLA-4 knockout mice all died due to sudden, exaggerated autoimmune responses by the time they were five weeks old.

Just when we became convinced that PD-1 could be an immune regulator, a 1996 paper by Jim Allison reported the successful treatment of cancer in mice by using anti-CTLA-4 antibodies. When we saw Dr. Allison's paper, we discussed how anti-CTLA-4 antibodies could not be applied to treatment in humans because blocking CTLA-4 triggers severe autoimmune disease. We were convinced that PD-1 was a far better target for cancer immunotherapy and therefore decided to continue experimenting with it.

Inhibition of PD-1 Suppresses Cancer Growth

Armed with this conviction about PD-1, a graduate student in my laboratory, Iwai Yoshiko (currently at Nippon Medical School), undertook an experiment in mice to test whether she could suppress tumor growth by using antibodies to inhibit PD-1. First, I had her conduct an experiment using PD-1 knockout mice because the effects of antibodies vary and because it is impossible to know whether a particular antibody will work well without actually trying it. When she implanted tumors in PD-1 knockout mice and compared tumor growth with that in normal (wild-type) mice, we were excited to find that the growth was clearly slower in the PD-1 knockout mice. Next, I wanted to test antibodies that inhibited signaling through PD-1. Using anti-PD-L1 antibodies that I received from Minato Nagahiro's laboratory, we discovered that they, too, suppressed tumor growth. In 2002, I raced to publish these findings.

At that time, there was a bright spotlight on the idea that PD-1 ligands on cancer cells suppress activation of lymphocytes and contribute to cancer cell proliferation. When we examined the effect of anti-PD-L1 antibodies on the ligand-expressing cancer cells, we found the antibodies to be incredibly effective. However, anti-PD-1 antibodies were also effective in preventing metastasis from the spleen to the liver in an experimental system using melanoma that does not express PD-L1. Subsequent analysis of patient data revealed that not all tumors express PD-1 ligands. In many studies, outcomes of anti-PD-1 antibody therapy did not always correlate with tumor ligand expression.

The Long and Winding Road to Commercial Development

Even before we published our 2002 paper, we thought that our research could lead to future application in humans, so we applied for a patent. However, we submitted the application just before Kyoto University was incorporated. Back then, the university's intellectual property department was unable to handle patent applications, so university researchers had to apply for patents on their own. Therefore, I turned to my former partner Ono Pharmaceutical for help with my patent application, which we filed jointly.

We applied for the patent before the paper was published; the filing of the patent application came a year and a half later. As soon as the paper was published, I encouraged Ono Pharmaceutical to begin developing anti-PD-1 antibodies. However, they had never worked with drugs for cancer and, with their limited capital resources, balked at the high financial risk of development, which could have cost them tens of billions of yen (hundreds of millions of dollars). To lessen the financial risk, representatives of Ono Pharmaceutical visited major pharmaceutical companies throughout Japan to propose joint development. They even consulted with the Japanese branch of an American pharmaceutical company. A year later, he brought me a list of all the companies he had approached and told me, "No one accepted our offer, so Ono Pharmaceutical can't help you with developing anti-PD-1 antibodies."

I couldn't bear to give up, so I decided to speak with an American friend who runs a venture-backed company. When I asked for his help with development, he immediately said yes—but on one condition: that Ono Pharmaceutical, the joint patent applicant, either relinquish its patent right or grant his company an exclusive license. When I spoke to Ono Pharmaceutical about releasing the claim, they said they wanted to think about it. About three or four months later, they told me that they were going to collaborate with me after all. At the time, I had no idea why they changed their mind and agreed to work with me to develop anti-PD-1 antibodies for clinical use, but I was unbelievably glad that they did. However, the reason that finally emerged was that Medarex, an American venture-backed company with the technology to produce human antibodies by using mice, had just entered a joint development agreement with Ono Pharmaceutical. Clinical trials of anti-PD-1 antibodies began in 2006.

Looking back, I can understand why so many major pharmaceutical companies hesitated to tackle development. As I discussed earlier, cancer immunotherapy had a horrible reputation in 2002 and 2003. Most cancer specialists were highly dubious about immunotherapy, and some even considered it a sham. That reputation stemmed from the fact that all the numerous and varied methods tested (cytokine therapy, vaccine therapy, adoptive immunotherapy, and whatever therapy immunologists proposed) had completely failed to yield noteworthy therapeutic effects in specific clinical settings. Contrary to the usual path that medical products follow to commercialization, the development of anti-PD-1 antibodies likely came to fruition only through the unusual connection between Ono Pharmaceutical, which had no experience in the clinical cancer field, and a venture-backed biotech company that could produce human antibodies.

Shocking Therapeutic Outcomes

Another bit of good fortune came in 2009, when Medarex was purchased by Bristol Myers Squibb; afterward, clinical trials progressed rapidly. The first trial began in 2006 to investigate safety. At that time, cancer immunotherapy was not widely accepted in the United States. Therefore, the patients who participated in the trial all had a terminal disease, were beyond the help of any treatment at any hospital, and signed up for the Phase I study as their last hope. Roughly 200 people with various large and advanced tumors (melanoma, lung cancer, renal-cell cancer, prostate cancer, and colon cancer) were the first patients to receive anti-PD-1 antibodies.

The trial's results appeared in presentations at various academic conferences, and rumors circulated that the therapy worked surprisingly well. In 2012, the trial culminated in a paper that ran in the *New England Journal of Medicine*. The results were absolutely shocking: anti-PD-1 immunotherapy achieved positive clinical benefits in roughly 20% to 30% of the patients with terminal cancer. The therapy demonstrated further groundbreaking results in patients with melanoma, lung cancer, and renal-cell cancer: after the patients received anti-PD-1 antibodies, their tumors either shrank or remained the same size—and the effect lasted for more than a year. These results made the front page of the *Wall Street Journal* and received substantial coverage in a German financial newspaper. Anti-PD-1 antibodies were billed as an unprecedented new method for treating cancer.

Clinical Trials Progress Rapidly

After this newspaper coverage, several more trials made progress. The first trial to make significant headway dealt with melanoma. As discussed earlier, a Phase III clinical trial that appeared in the *New England Journal of Medicine* in 2014 divided roughly 400 participants into two groups: one received anti-PD-1 antibodies, and the other received an anticancer drug called dacarbazine, which was then considered to be the most potent drug for the treatment of melanoma. One year later, 70% of the patients who had received anti-PD-1 antibodies were still alive, compared with a survival rate of just 35% among those who received dacarbazine. Furthermore, after 15 months, the percentage of survivors in the anti-PD-1 antibody group remained steady at 70%, whereas the survival rate in the dacarbazine group had fallen to a mere 20%. At this point, the trial was discontinued for ethical reasons.

In collaboration with the Kyoto University Department of Gynecology and Obstetrics, we conducted a Phase II trial to assess the efficacy of anti-PD-1 antibodies in the treatment of ovarian cancer. Of the 20 patients in the trial, three demonstrated remarkable clinical effects and experience no subsequent recurrence of their disease. Another six patients saw their tumors remain the same size, which I consider a therapeutic effect of a sort. In ovarian cancer, prognoses are typically poor. The patients who participated in this trial were already undergoing treatment with platinum-based drugs, had experienced recurrence, or were otherwise out of options. Therefore, the fact that 9 of the 20 patients demonstrated responses, regardless of their magnitude, astonished the clinician community.

Having shown such spectacular efficacy, anti-PD-1 antibodies received approval in the United States for melanoma in 2014 and for lung cancer and renal-cell cancer in 2015. As (Table 1, page 33) indicates, anti-PD-1 antibodies have secured approval in Japan for melanoma and lung cancer and, later, for renal-cell cancer and Hodgkin lymphoma. Nearly 1000 clinical trials for anti-PD-1 antibodies have been registered on the United States National Institutes of Health website, and ongoing clinical trials are investigating an incredibly wide variety of tumors. Going forward, anti-PD-1 antibodies will likely be applied to an increasingly longer list of tumors.

A Series of Fortunate Events

I believe that we owe the discovery of PD-1 to a series of fortunate events. First, the encounter with the molecule was serendipitous. Because we persisted in our research despite countless struggles, we learned that PD-1 acts as an immune system brake. In addition, we were able to develop a laboratory mouse model that was potentially applicable in cancer therapy. Our attempts at development also encountered all kinds of difficulties, but Medarex ultimately elected to work with us. Furthermore, although the reasons remain a mystery, anti-PD-1 antibodies were effective more often in humans than in our laboratory mouse model.

At first, even I was doubtful that PD-1 could be turned into an anticancer target. In the life sciences, things rarely go according to calculation. The discovery of PD-1 is symbolic of that. Sometimes, various basic experiments eventually end up producing results that lead to clinical application. Is that not the essence of scientific research? No one knows which seeds will grow into trees that bear fruit. The important thing is to try many seeds—basic experiments—and see what happens.

Future Issues in Anti-PD-1 Antibody Therapy

PD-1 Provides a Breakthrough

As I mentioned earlier, anti-PD-1 antibody therapy represented a profound change in the conventional notions of treating cancer and the start of a new era in cancer immunotherapy.

An article in the 5 March 2016 issue of *New Scientist* opined that the development of anti-PD-1 antibody therapy for cancer was on par with the discovery of penicillin, which paved the way for a novel concept of treating infections. Although penicillin alone cannot prevent all infections, the discoveries of antibiotics that followed has enabled humanity to achieve control over infections and, in some cases, conquer them. Although the cancer immunotherapy breakthrough provided by PD-1 has generated anticipation regarding its future application in treating many types of cancer, many issues remain.

The Characteristics of Anti-PD-1 Antibody Therapy

There are three main characteristics of cancer therapy using anti-PD-1 antibodies. First, anti-PD-1 antibodies are effective in an incredibly wide variety of cancers. In fact, anti-PD-1 antibodies are likely to achieve some degree of effectiveness in the majority of carcinomas (cancers of the skin or linings or coverings of internal organs). Second, once anti-PD-1 antibodies begin to work in a patient, the effects last for several years. If the tumor begins to grow again after several years, additional anti-PD-1 antibody therapy is possible. Third, anti-PD-1 immunotherapy causes relatively few side effects. One key concern is the potential development of autoimmune diseases. However, with careful observation, doctors can perform appropriate treatment before an autoimmune disease becomes severe.

Based on these characteristics, anti-PD-1 antibody therapy stands to be one of the first-line treatments for cancer in the future. However, the therapy still faces several unresolved key issues.

Some Patients Do Not Respond to the Therapy

The first hurdle regarding anti-PD-1 antibody therapy is that some patients do not respond to treatment. For example, in melanoma, the therapy yields no effect in roughly 30% of patients. For other cancers, as many as half of patients may not respond. Many researchers are aware of this problem and are searching for a solution. But what can be done for these so-called non-responders? A couple of new anticancer regimens under investigation combine anti-PD-1 antibody therapy with either a different method that further inhibits another type of immune brake, low-dose chemotherapy, or low-dose radiation therapy. Despite these efforts, the non-responder issue remains unresolved and therefore continues to be an object of scrutiny for many researchers and pharmaceutical companies.

These individual differences in responses to anti-PD-1 immunotherapy stem from the diversity of the immune system. For example, some people have an allergic response to a given substance, whereas other people do not. Hay fever afflicts some but not all. The same goes for immune reactions to different pollens. As these examples show, immune responses differ wildly from person to person.

Distinguishing between Responders and Non-responders in Advance

Another major challenge in anti-PD-1 immunotherapy is finding a method for distinguishing between non-responders and likely responders before the administration of anti-PD-1 antibodies.

Anti-PD-1 antibody therapy takes at least three months, typically six months, and sometimes one year. The only way to know whether the therapy will work is to actually try it, a limitation that affects the patient's quality of life. In addition, the therapy imposes burdens on healthcare staff, increases medical expenses, and generates many forms of waste. To avoid these problems, many researchers are currently devoting a great deal of effort to searching for markers that distinguish responders from non-responders.

As I touched on earlier, the initial idea was that because the expression of PD-1 ligands is a major trigger of tumor growth, stopping (or interfering with) this PD-L1-to-PD-1 signaling is the key to anti-PD-1 immunotherapy. However, detailed examination of real-world clinical cases has demonstrated that the percentage of tumors expressing PD-1 ligands does not clearly correlate with the efficacy of anti-PD-1 immunotherapy. Currently, many researchers are striving to find a better marker.

Drug Prices

Another key problem comes from a different perspective: anti-PD-1 antibodies are more expensive than conventional anticancer agents.

Drug prices are set differently in different countries. For example, pharmaceutical companies in the United States set prices on their own (in negotiation with insurance companies) and then leave the rest to market selection. In Japan, by contrast, discussions among representatives of insurers, patients, and physicians in the Central Social Insurance Medical Council determine drug prices in light of cost accounting and other factors.

Some in the media have criticized anti-PD-1 antibodies, claiming that their ridiculously expensive prices would cause healthcare fees to skyrocket and collapse the Japanese social insurance system. However, this argument requires careful examination. The development of an effective therapy will discourage the use of outdated, ineffective therapies, which should eliminate the corresponding healthcare fees. Conventional cancer therapy generally requires the hospitalization of patients, who undergo treatment for months and possibly years; comparisons of healthcare fees must weigh the expenses of those hospitalization periods. In addition, most conventional cancer therapies were expected to prolong the patient's life by 6 to 12 months. However, if anti-PD-1 antibodies can be administered on an outpatient basis for three to six months and achieve complete remission or semi-permanently prevent tumor growth, the associated reduction in healthcare costs would be immense.

Furthermore, the Japanese Ministry of Health, Labour and Welfare is already moving forward with a system that reduces the price of any medical product with a sales turnover of over ¥100 billion (roughly USD936 million). As PD-1 antibodies are applied to a wider range of cancers, their price will likely decrease. Therefore, at this point in time, the criticism regarding the price of anti-PD-1 antibodies has no quantitative basis whatsoever. Any discussion of drug prices must thoroughly examine cost-effectiveness.

The Speed of Application Expansion

Currently, anti-PD-1 immunotherapy is used to treat melanoma, ovarian cancer, non-small-cell lung cancer, and renal-cell cancer. Going forward, anti-PD-1 antibodies will likely find applications in a wider variety of cancers. But how will the next cancer for anti-PD-1 immunotherapy be chosen? Most patients want anti-PD-1 antibodies to be applied to their own type of cancer as soon as possible. Pharmaceutical companies presumably set their priorities based on multiple perspectives: the size of the market, favorable outcomes in clinical trials, and, of course, patient needs.

The difficulty here is that conducting complete Phase II and Phase III clinical trials of anti-PD-1 antibodies for every single type of cancer would take years. Whether applications can somehow be expanded more quickly is an issue for healthcare administration, and demands from patients are likely to become increasingly forceful.

Controlling Side Effects

Although anti-PD-1 antibody therapy has few side effects, they are not completely absent. The most important aspect of managing the side effects of anti-PD-1 antibody therapy is for physicians to check vigilantly for the onset of autoimmune disease.

Currently, clinical cancer specialists remain largely unfamiliar with immunotherapy. Therefore, anti-PD-1 antibodies can only be used at hospitals where specialists in clinical immunology are present to work with cancer specialists. The time will soon come when cancer specialists themselves are knowledgeable in immunity and can effectively monitor and address patients' side effects—but until then, cancer specialists will require the support of immunologists.

One tricky thing about autoimmune diseases is that it is impossible to predict which organs a disease will affect in a given patient. The most common autoimmune diseases, by far, are interstitial pneumonia, enteritis, arthritis, dermatitis, and nephritis. However, countless other diseases fall into the autoimmune disease category. By closely monitoring patients to avoid missing any signs of autoimmune disease, physicians can prevent autoimmune diseases from becoming severe, treating them and cancer at the same time.

Individual differences determine which patients develop autoimmune diseases and the organs in which diseases manifest. Hundreds of genes associated with the immune system determine various characteristics, such as the conditions of the immune system's activation, diversity in antigen recognition, and the level of production of inflammatory-response-triggering cytokines. Even if all humans were to have the same set of genes, with different combinations of polymorphisms (sequence variations) of those genes, different levels of gene expression would still yield incredibly different responses. When an immune response is too powerful, the attack on a specific organ intensifies, thereby triggering autoimmune disease.

Therefore, when a person with a preexisting autoimmune disease develops cancer, physicians tend to be reluctant to recommend anti-PD-1 antibody therapy. However, I believe that anti-PD-1 immunotherapy accommodates concurrent anticancer treatment and the management of autoimmune disease even in these patients.

The Importance of Basic Research: Thinking about the Relationship between Academia and Business

A New Competition Begins

In 2016, the United States government launched the Cancer Moonshot, a large-scale federal cancer treatment project headed by then-Vice President Joe Biden. The following year, the Cancer Moonshot was appropriated USD 1 billion in funding. Cancer immunotherapy was established as one of the pillars of this project. In addition, philanthropists have been donating hundreds of millions of dollars to found cancer immunotherapy labs and launch new research centers at myriad universities.

Despite being the birthplace of anti-PD-1 antibody therapy, Japan has not yet shown broad, exuberant philanthropic or governmental support of cancer immunotherapy like the backing it has received in the United States. Earlier, I cited a claim that put anti-PD-1 antibody therapy on par with penicillin. The discovery of penicillin made it possible to conquer infection, but not all infections can be cured with penicillin. In the same manner, PD-1 needs to serve as the spark to clear a path to the next stages of development. The United States views PD-1 as a first step and has begun moving forward.

Although the race to make effective use of anti-PD-1 antibody therapy has begun, Japan is still standing awkwardly near the starting line. The PD-1 breakthrough is a new horizon toward which everyone else is running, but Japan is apparently oblivious that the pursuit has even started. Japan should invest in PD-1 development to attract more researchers and expand research efforts.

Breakthroughs Cannot Be Designed

Looking back at the history of PD-1 research, not even I ever dreamed in the initial post-discovery phase that it would lead to drugs that would be effective against cancer.

PD-1 has an incredibly unique structure, and its expression is extremely localized—characteristics that make it an intriguing molecule and have propelled research. After nearly 10 years, the research bore its first fruit: PD-1 was shown to be involved in the inhibitory regulation of immunity. This finding led us to consider that PD-1 might be useful in cancer therapy. When we tested the approach, it worked incredibly well. Another 10 years later, the cancer therapeutic effect observed in animal models was reproduced in humans. Currently, anti-PD-1 antibodies are used as pharmaceutical products worldwide. As this history shows, major breakthroughs in life sciences cannot be planned or designed.

Take the auspicious Apollo Project, a groundbreaking feat of engineering that started in 1961 when United States President John F. Kennedy declared his intentions to put humans on the moon. Thanks to elaborate planning and vast amounts of funding, the project succeeded. After Kennedy, in 1971, President Nixon proposed the War on Cancer as the next federal project. With the goal of defeating cancer in five years (1976, the United States' bicentennial year), the War on Cancer received a staggering amount of research funding. However, the project failed to achieve its perhaps overly ambitious goal.

In other words, some projects proceed according to a clear road map to the outcome. Rockets, bridges, and tunnels, for example, often arrive at completion according to plan. Pharmaceutical products, meanwhile, tend to yield results based on fortuitous findings from life-science research. These two kinds of projects should be considered as having fundamentally different personalities.

The Characteristics of Life-Science Research

A great deal of life-science research involves things that cannot be known unless they are actually tried. In life-science research, I feel that it is necessary to sow as many seeds as possible. For example, using anti-PD-1 antibodies as anticancer immunotherapy started with my research, even though I am not a cancer researcher.

If you sow 10,000 seeds, maybe a fifth of them will sprout. Only a fraction of the seeds that sprout will grow into full plants. Again, only a fraction of those plants will bear fruit. And even if they do, only some of those fruits will taste good. Ultimately, it is entirely possible that you will get only a few trees that bear good fruit from a planting of 10,000 seeds.

As I have described, the process of attempting to turn life-science research into fruit (pharmaceutical agents) is, to put it plainly, a gamble. Success hinges, therefore, on sowing lots of seeds—basic studies—a process that needs to be taken seriously. I feel that anyone who fails to heed this point should not approach researchers in the life sciences with a five-year project, no matter what disease the project intends to cure.

Digging Deeper into Basic Studies and Turning Them into Products

We need the ability to determine which basic studies will bear fruit. We also need to be able to identify "good fruit" and grow only the trees that bear the best results.

These goals entail several steps. The first step is to dig deeply into the diverse variety of basic studies, those that provide the foundational knowledge that people can apply practically to solve problems. All life-science researchers work tirelessly on basic studies. The second step—identifying and cultivating fruit that might be good—means developing those basic results into pharmaceutical agents and other products. The first part of this step involves the assessment of basic research conducted primarily at universities and the world of academia. In the second part of this step, the baton passes from academia to business, which identifies findings that could turn into real-world products.

This product-development step is currently regarded as supremely important in Japan, and many schemes to develop new products have been launched. Unfortunately, however, the process has not been going smoothly. In addition, going full-speed ahead on only the second step will cause the fruit to run out quickly. Bearing lots of fruit requires a big-picture view in which both of the two steps above are emphasized and pursued as two parts of a whole.

An Eye for Seeds

According to one report, Japanese businesses strongly favor working with non-Japanese universities over investing in seeds of research from Japanese universities. I think this is a tragedy. Despite the outstanding seeds that Japanese universities have created, Japanese companies seem to have few people with an eye for those seeds.

Large companies in particular are reluctant to speculate with their investments. Many employees at large companies take a very measured, cautious perspective; fearing failure, they tend not to want to gamble. As I stated earlier, there is an aspect of gambling in the research and development of pharmaceutical agents. Without the willingness to try the new and unconventional, revolutionary products will never emerge. This is why the West places such immense importance on venture-backed companies, which have a mechanism for approaching challenges without having to risk a company's future on a "high risk, high reward" mindset. This mechanism provides an opportunity for young people with big dreams to pursue those aspirations with investments from venture capitalists.

In Japan, many people do not know how they should use their wealth. The fact that someone who suddenly comes into money would mindlessly buy up hoards of extremely expensive wine shows that many potential investors never pause to consider how they might invest their money to benefit humanity. How incredibly unfortunate.

Cultivating the Seeds of the Next Generation

When I consider the future of Japanese pharmaceutical companies, I feel that firms need to do more than just follow the current trend of commercializing seeds from academia via venture-backed companies to produce major results. Reinforcing the one-way mechanism in which seeds from academia are transferred to business does nothing to avert a Japanese future in which these seeds would eventually be depleted. Government and business need to establish an effective system in which corporate wealth—the product of seeds from academia—finds its way back to academia.

In Japan, universities today are strapped for cash due to factors such as cuts in subsidies for management expenses. This lack of funds disproportionately affects young researchers. I feel that if things continue as they are, the future of Japan is incredibly bleak. Ever since national universities were incorporated, they have been in decline on the world stage in terms of the numbers of papers published and numerous other indicators.

The PD-1 protein was identified in 1992, and its anticancer effect was discovered in 2002, just before the incorporation of national universities in Japan. Therefore, the results we are seeing now for anti-PD-1 immunotherapy can be considered to have sprung from the relatively fertile environment that existed before universities were incorporated. What will the environment be like 10 years from now? We will have to keep a close eye on what transpires.

I propose that the commercial fruit born of academic research seeds should not only be reinvested into business but also that a sufficient percentage be invested in academia, which needs money to produce the next generation of seeds. The research on PD-1 took place at Kyoto University. It was the work of Kyoto University researchers. I have long thought that the fruits of our research should be returned to Kyoto University so that our young researchers can pursue promising leads without worrying about funding for 10 years or so. With the money I received for my Nobel Prize in Physiology or Medicine, donations from the general public, and the patent royalties I will receive for the drug Opdivo, I have established the Tasuku Honjo "Yuh-shi" Fund at Kyoto University. This fund brings our dream for our young researchers closer to reality.

The Future of the Japanese Pharmaceutical Industry

I believe that the Japanese pharmaceutical industry needs a major shake-up. The top Japanese pharmaceutical company ranks only 16th among pharmaceutical companies worldwide. About 20 pharmaceutical companies around the globe are considered to be capable of developing new drugs and marketing them internationally. Although the Japanese pharmaceutical industry is crowded with many companies, almost none of them currently have a global sales network or the capacity to supply new drugs worldwide.

If Japan's pharmaceutical companies fail to undergo major consolidation and continue to be unable to develop Japanese seeds globally, they likely will be merged into other, internationally equipped companies. Policies to protect domestic industry might steer Japan away from that fate, but the Japanese people would likely incur high costs. Previously, as part of the so-called "convoy system" under the management of the Ministry of Health, Labour and Welfare, pharmaceutical companies were forced to set high drug prices so that they could survive even if they never ventured outside the domestic market. However, this policy was partially responsible for the sharp rise in social welfare costs.

If academic institutions and pharmaceutical companies in Japan cannot share in a win-win relationship, what will happen? One possibility is that Japanese pharmaceutical companies will remain unable to compete internationally and will be weeded out. Another possibility is that Japanese researchers will partner with non-Japanese pharmaceutical companies. Those in academia have realized that they have far more to gain by partnering with non-Japanese pharmaceutical companies that can expand research results on an international scale than by collaborating with their Japanese counterparts. Therefore, if Japanese pharmaceutical companies fail to forge a win-win relationship with academia, they face a bleak future.

What Is Life?

Research on life has taught us many new ways of thinking. Life itself is, to begin with, philosophy and thought.

The idea that biology gave birth to and that has had the greatest effect on society is Darwin's theory of evolution. Today, mutation (reformation), competition, and evolution are the fundamental lenses for viewing all social phenomena on earth. Sadly, in the United States, the theory of evolution continues to foment educational battles because of religious reasons. Overall, however, there is no doubt that the theory of evolution has become firmly established in human thought worldwide.

The second major idea regarding life is Mendelian inheritance. Although traits were widely known to be hereditary, it was previously thought that a child's traits were the "averages" of their parents' factors, which somehow mixed together. But as Mendel laboriously researched pea plants by himself at a Czech monastery, his analyses showed that genetic traits are passed down to descendants through "particles" (later identified to be genes) that do not mix together. However, the idea that genes are shared by humanity did not take root until much later. In the early twentieth century, research on chromosomes by Hugo de Vries and Thomas Hunt Morgan confirmed the laws of Mendelian inheritance, which society finally embraced.

The theory of evolution and Mendelian inheritance are still the fundamental axioms of biology today and therefore have greatly affected how people live in society. However, the general public has yet to recognize the significance of these two axioms in full. Thus, their influence obviously needs a more detailed explanation.

What I want to emphasize is this: the second half of the twentieth century saw a shift from biology to life science—that is, from a focus on living organisms in their immediate environment to a broader view of life and its interactions at levels from the subcellular to cosmic. This explosion of development in life science highlighted a new understanding of organisms. In turn, this understanding introduced a new perspective into biology and therefore into general thought that differed from the physics-based world-view that once formed the foundation of natural science.

Life science continues to demonstrate dynamic development. I anticipate that this new understanding of "the way organisms should be," or "the principle of life" shaping this new life science, will be integrated into a more unified concept and serve as a foundation for future development in life science.

By demonstrating a new ideal for organisms, life science has affected society in unexpected ways. Discord has emerged between life science and conventional sociocultural thought, raising major issues in social thought and ethics.

For example, developments in reproductive medicine have compelled us to redefine the parent-child relationship. Regenerative medicine leads us to view human beings as collections of replaceable parts, forcing us to reconsider issues such as human dignity and the finite nature of life. Advancements in brain research may result in science determining the nature of consciousness, which had always been the domain of philosophy. This advancement in life science may be too shocking for some people to accept, and they may not want to hear about it.

What should life science try to achieve? What will the astonishing developments in life science lead us to discover? Life science already has strong associations with philosophy and social thought. In this chapter, I would like to change gears a bit and consider "living" and "life" through the lens of life science.

The Biology of Happiness

The Origin of Happiness

Everyone wants to be happy. The question of what happiness is, however, has been a philosophical quandary since the time of Aristotle. The problem of how to define "happy" has captured our attention throughout 3000 years of civilization.

I have no intention of discussing philosophical arguments here. However, all philosophers have agreed that the feeling of happiness is fundamentally pleasurable. Pleasure is the fulfillment of a desire: appetite, sex drive, and the acquisition of power (competition), for example.

To get a scientific understanding of why the fulfillment of desire brings pleasure, it is useful to consider the converse.

If eating did not bring humans pleasure, what would happen? If humans do not eat, they die. Arousing the desire to eat is essential to an organism's survival.

Without a sex drive, we could not produce descendants. A sex drive is thus essential for life to continue beyond the individual. Without a sex drive, we would not exist.

The desire for power (competition) likely stems from the pleasure of victory over an enemy. Without this feeling of pleasure, organisms would not fight; instead, they would spend their lives running from their enemies. In other words, organisms would not last long in the struggle for survival.

This perspective reveals that the factors that bring humans pleasure are necessary for survival. Into these factors, organisms likely incorporated sensations (recognition mechanisms) that lead to the pleasure center of the brain, thus linking these factors to prerequisites for survival. The species that are still alive today are those that have succeeded at this incorporation.

Considering that the history of life on earth stretches back 3.6 billion years, it is no surprise that humans exist today. The Darwinian idea that evolution progresses according to both chance genetic mutations and the selection of the resulting traits according to the environment of the population is an unshakable truth supported by molecular biological data. Happiness is also a product of evolution.

Evolution Gives Rise to Morality

Some may object to the idea of bringing a biological perspective to a philosophical issue like happiness. However, if life science were not assessed correctly—even in different fields like the humanities and social sciences—not only would new developments cease to occur, but major errors could also be made. Just as it is with the issue of happiness, it is important that the results of progress in life science continue to be evaluated through the lenses of the humanities and social sciences.

For example, some believe that moral behavior and sympathy for others are advanced characteristics exclusive to humans. In religious thought, the dominant belief is that morality is a special trait that developed in humans to awaken them from their wild nature and make them social.

However, we can observe similar characteristics in other primates, which have close evolutionary ties to humans. For example, bonobos (pygmy chimpanzees) and chimpanzees live in groups numbering in the dozens and display sympathetic behavior and cooperation among their fellow group members. These trends are particularly prominent in bonobos, which molecular biology research suggests are genetically closer to humans than are chimpanzees.

Why do bonobos demonstrate altruistic behavior? From an evolutionary standpoint, helping members of one's group is essential for the survival of a group comprising few individuals. Tending to the injured and sharing food ensures the survival of both the group and the individual. Groups comprising non-altruistic individuals, therefore, will fail to survive.

Expanding on the idea of the evolutionary biologist Theodosius Dobzhansky, who stated that "Nothing in biology makes sense except in the light of evolution," the primatologist Frans de Waal believes that moral behaviors are not unique to humans, are necessary for organisms to survive, and, from a rational perspective, are likely the product of selection. However, humans indisputably also display a unique culture-based sense of morality.

Chance and Necessity

The results of evolution have rational explanations, but they are difficult to predict. Temporal constraints limit the range of species on which scientists can perform experiments, for instance. Evolution occurs by chance, and much is unknown regarding which mutations will affect the various properties of humans as a species. But in some cases, we have incredibly detailed knowledge regarding the background of a certain property.

For example, in red blood cells, the mutation of a single base in the hemoglobin β-chain gene changes the glutamate residue to valine, thereby changing the molecular structure of hemoglobin and, consequently, the shape of red blood cells. Thus, this point mutation triggers a recessive disorder called "sickle cell disease," in which red blood cells easily get stuck in capillaries, resulting in the destruction of red blood cells and, consequently, anemia.

However, people who have this mutation in only one of the two chromosomes carrying the gene are resistant to malaria. As a result, the distribution of people with sickle cell disease genes overlaps strikingly with the distribution of the parasite that causes malaria, extending from Africa to the Middle East and from the Mediterranean coast to India. In regions where malaria is prevalent, therefore, having a chromosome that carries the sickle cell gene confers a survival advantage. However, the sickle cell gene has different effects in different geographical areas. For the descendants of Africans who were forcibly taken to North America, where malaria does not exist, the sickle cell gene causes anemia and confers no survival benefit whatsoever. Sickle cell disease is an excellent example of how a change in environment has a major bearing on the roles and significance of genes.

Another good example is diabetes. Humans first emerged in an environment where food was always limited. In those circumstances, organisms emphasized mechanisms that increase blood glucose and incorporated these mechanisms into their genetic makeup. The environmental changes that have transpired since—going from food scarcity to food prevalence—are presumed to be an underlying cause of diabetes.

Although anemia and diabetes seem disadvantageous at first glance, they were selected as beneficial mechanisms for survival in a past environment. The most rational understanding of how organisms have achieved their current forms is that they incorporated mutations that facilitated survival in the environments they inhabited.

The Genes That Govern Happiness

If pleasure and happiness are the products of evolution, they likely have a genetic basis, as do other mechanisms in organisms. Regarding appetite, the substance called "ghrelin" gives a pleasure stimulus when an organism eats after feeling hungry. Ghrelin, which was discovered in 1999 by Professor Kangawa Kenji of the National Cerebral and Cardiovascular Center in Osaka, is a peptide hormone that comprises 28 amino acids. Ghrelin is secreted from the stomach into the blood, where it is received by neurons (which have receptors for ghrelin). These receptors, which are expressed predominantly in the hypothalamus, are believed to enhance the pleasure gained from eating by stimulating the secretion of neuropeptide Y, which then stimulates the brain's reward pathway (the pathway that brings pleasure) and triggers the release of dopamine. In contrast, fat cells secrete the peptide called "leptin," which reduces appetite. In leptin-deficient mice, appetite is not suppressed, causing the mice to get fat.

Similar to those modulating appetite, several substances are known to control sex drive. For example, we know that, through the molecules called "pheromones," animals detect the presence of individuals of the opposite sex, and they are believed to exist in humans as well. In addition, sex hormones are secreted in conjunction with sexual maturity and unmistakably control sex drive in humans and other organisms.

Adrenaline, which is secreted by sympathetic nerves and the adrenal glands, regulates the competitive response associated with the desire for power. Adrenaline receptors are widely distributed in the brain, heart, and muscles; the stimulation of these receptors activates the metabolism, accelerates the heartbeat, and increases muscle strength. This mechanism is incredibly effective in preparing the entire body to fight when an enemy is encountered.

The Numbing of Sensations

As has long been known, the pleasure that humans feel, regulated by substances such as those described above, eventually wanes.

Back when sugar was a valuable commodity, the philosopher Jean-Jacques Rousseau is said to have noted that drinking sugared water every day would gradually diminish its subjective flavor. Therefore, the best way to prolong the pleasurable experience was by gradually increasing the concentration of sugar in the water every day. After increasing the concentration of sugar to its peak, Rousseau noted that it was good to forego sugar for a while and then start over with a low concentration to again enjoy its sweetness.

As the sugar example shows, the major problem with happiness based on pleasure is that it will eventually be blunted. This numbing of happiness is consistent with the biological phenomenon in which continued stimulation of a receptor eventually blunts that receptor's responsiveness—in other words, desensitizes the receptor.

Another Factor: Anxiety

As philosophers have indicated, the mere fulfillment of desires does not yield true happiness. There is another potential factor in happiness: the absence of anxiety.

What causes anxiety? When do humans feel fear? Of course, we feel afraid when our existence is threatened. The thought of possibly dying from illness makes everyone anxious. More than that, we feel a fear beyond words when something attacks us and threatens our lives. We also feel anxious when food is scarce, given the potential for starvation. According to psychology research, our anxiety intensifies when noises in the darkness occur more frequently and get louder. Obviously, these phenomena make us anxious because we associate them with the approach of an enemy. Therefore, the greatest cause of anxiety is the sense of difficulty in fulfilling our desire to live.

So why have we inherited this anxiety? The answer is obvious: without anxiety, we would not attempt to fight or flee desperately enough when our lives were in danger, thus decreasing our chances for survival.

Generally speaking, anxiety is correlated with unpleasantness and rooted in the unfulfillment of desire. However, there are various levels of anxiety. For example, someone who has never experienced misfortune would be upset by even the most trivial things, whereas someone who has experienced extreme misfortune, such as someone who has narrowly avoided being killed, would want for almost nothing as long as they were alive. The level of anxiety relief also differs remarkably depending on the experience. Perhaps the threshold for anxiety has a correlation to the minimal requisite level for the desire to live. The Buddhist monk Shinran said, "Even a good person can be reborn in the Pure Land; how much more easily an evil person!"—meaning that an "evil" person recognizes their own weakness and seeks salvation by faith. A newer interpretation of Shinran's words holds that because "evil" people have had many experiences and are thus less likely to feel that their lives are threatened by minor things, their threshold for anxiety is higher, thereby leading them to salvation.

This sort of change in sensitivity threshold is supported by clear biological evidence. Usher syndrome is a genetic disease in which sensory abnormalities gradually occur after birth. As a result, patients who have lost their sight and hearing are said to develop a strikingly keen sense of smell. This shows that experiences produce feedback to the sensory center, causing thresholds to fluctuate. In patients with Usher syndrome, the loss of other sensory signals likely amplifies sensitivity (that is, reduces the threshold) to olfactory signals.

I believe that humanity came up with a great invention to attain happiness without anxiety: religion. In my opinion, the most important role of religion is to provide a program for relieving all sorts of worries and anxieties. Seemingly built into every religion is a mechanism by which followers can obtain a sense of security by submitting and completely devoting themselves to an absolute power.

Biologically, the existence of two types of happiness—the fulfillment of desire and the elimination of anxiety—is consistent with previous philosophical consideration. From this point of view, the road to eternal happiness is likely a mixture of peace of mind and occasional pleasurable stimuli. Perhaps the happiest way to spend one's later years is to live in serenity while sometimes enjoying a pastime, like golf or fine dining.

Genome Imperialism

Physics Imperialism and The History of Life Science

Around 1960, when I entered university, physics was considered the most eminent discipline in the natural sciences (and may still be considered so). From Newtonian dynamics to the theory of relativity, physics is a deductive science in which everything is represented by mathematical expressions. It perhaps goes without saying that physics has been the driving force behind the natural sciences. For people engaged in physics research back then, it was natural to think that physics defined the framework of natural sciences and that the principles of physics could explain all natural phenomena. We aspiring biologists ridiculed this domineering physics-centric thinking as "physics imperialism."

By the 1960s, DNA had at last been determined to carry genetic information, and work was underway to unravel the principles of the genetic code. However, life science involves a great deal of "fuzziness," and the majority of life-science research was confined to descriptions of phenomena. It is perfectly understandable that life science was viewed as backward and antiquated by people studying physics.

Also during the 1960s, many people believed that organisms were largely shrouded in mystery—a belief that is likely still strong today. However, the discovery of the double-helical structure of DNA by James Watson and Francis Crick in 1953 established that genes, the basis of life phenomena, had a material foundation. In the latter half of the twentieth century, molecular biology revealed the material basis of life phenomena. As a result, all life phenomena broke out of the realm of mystery, and the idea that matter sustains life phenomena entered the mainstream. This unraveling of life phenomena culminated in the sequencing of the entire human genome, which was announced in 2003. Complete genomes have also been obtained not only for *E. coli* and yeast but also for other representative species, including mice, fruit flies, zebrafish, and rice plants as well as chimpanzees, opossums, and the aforementioned Dr. Watson himself. With DNA sequencing methods becoming ever faster and cheaper, genomic sequences will likely become available for entire species and individual organisms, even.

Life as an Assembly of Information

Not only has the sequencing of the human genome had an incalculable effect on academic research itself in life science, but its social significance will also gradually earn recognition.

The first element of that significance is that determination of the complete picture of genetic information has revealed that just under 30,000 genes determine protein structures in humans, and this number is not vastly different from that for fruit flies. The latest estimate of protein-encoding genes in humans is even lower—20,488 genes. This finding has changed our perception of organisms from simple mishmashes of matter to complexes beautifully integrated by information that regulates function through the expression and elimination of matter.

The information that makes up an organism is broadly divided into two categories: genetic information engraved into DNA, first of all, and information acquired after birth, including memories cached in the brain due to experiences and immune system memories associated with the various pathogens that the organism has encountered. Illness can therefore be considered as a state of maladjustment of bio-information, in which abnormal acquired information has accumulated in response to conflicts with the various environments to which the organism is exposed after birth. This conception of illness suggests that an organism is, more accurately, an assembly of information that combines acquired information with a foundation of genetic information from DNA.

The protein molecules that compose an organism are all defined within the base sequence of the genome. Other molecules, like lipids and carbohydrates, are made by proteins. The second element of significance running through the sequencing of the human genome is the understanding that organisms operate within a limited framework. In physics, it is impossible to determine whether something does not exist or cannot be measured. In life science, however, it can be asserted that something that is not present in genomic information is not present in the organism. If so, are organisms—composed of limited information—simpler than the phenomena that physics covers? On the contrary, the molecules and information contained within organisms are likely far more complex than anything in physics, as I will explain later.

The sequencing of the human genome holds a third sense of significance for society: the notion that comparisons with the genomes of animals such as chimpanzees will soon reveal the genes that make us human and the mechanisms that regulate them. The genetic differences between humans and chimpanzees have always been predicted to be miniscule. In addition, now that genomes can be sequenced for individual people, we might soon be discussing the basis of individuality and personality at the genetic level. The significance of this development for society and the humanities is immense.

The Two "Principles" of Life Science

It would not be an overstatement to say that only two fundamental principles have been demonstrated in life science.

The first principle is Mendelian inheritance. The laws of Mendelian inheritance, which explain how the genetic information in DNA is passed down from parents to children through the generations, have definitively been proven by modern molecular biology. This principle holds that an organism is inevitably defined by the genetic information it inherits from its parents.

The second principle is Darwinian evolution. This principle corresponds to the so-called "survival of the fittest": the notion that genetic information undergoes random mutations, and advantageous traits resulting from those mutations are selected by the environment. This principle describes randomness—specifically how random mutations in genetic information are distributed among a group in their random environment and how those mutations affect the formation of a species over long periods of time.

Therefore, both of these principles of life science tie into the manner in which descendants inherit genetic information.

Chance in Evolution

In the molecular biological explication of life phenomena, which is consolidated in the sequencing of the genome, one crucial point worth considering is that although the principles of life science do not run counter to the principles of physics or chemistry, the principles used in life science are not derived a priori from physics or chemistry. This is because genomic information is not derived inevitably from the principles of physics or chemistry but, as Jacques Monod stated, exists as it does today due to a combination of chance and necessity.

There are many examples of mechanisms in organisms that depend on the randomness of evolution. I cannot name them all here, but I will describe the most striking example: the origin of crystallins, which are transparent, stable proteins found in the lenses of eyes. The origins of crystallin molecules involve no systematic connections whatsoever among species. In addition, these molecules were selected for reasons completely unrelated to their original functions. For example, the lens of a duck's eye is filled with enzymes such as lactate dehydrogenase and enolase. In chickens, however, these enzymes are substituted with argininosuccinate lyase. Why did lenses come to be filled with enzymes such as these? Although we do not understand the answer to that question completely, what we do know is that lens proteins likely need to be transparent, stable, copiously produced, and free of precipitation and toxicity at high concentrations. Enzymatic activity with any other conditions was completely unnecessary. This suggests that proteins produced by chance in the cells of lens tissue were selected by chance.

Another example is the evolution of rhodopsin and opsins, which act as light sensors in the eyes. It is peculiar that the first of these proteins to appear in organisms was an opsin that recognizes red and green. After this opsin came rhodopsin, a photoreceptor that recognizes dark and light (that is, black and white). Thus, unlike television, color vision came first, followed by black and white vision.

Furthermore, all primates until the New World species were nocturnal and therefore temporarily lost their color receptor genes. However, when apes evolved further and became diurnal, receptor genes for color recognition recovered their function.

Bio-information has been ruled by chance from the beginning. In the genetic code, the four bases adenine (A), guanine (G), cytosine (C), and thymine (T) form triplet code units that determine amino acid sequences, which in turn determine the structures and functions of proteins.

Why did the bases A, G, C, and T become the basis for the genetic code in the first place? It is believed that a great deal of chance was involved. In addition, the correspondence of base triplets to amino acids is not thought to involve any particular rationale. In all likelihood, a primitive organism born eons ago acquired a mechanism that linked these nucleic acid sequences to an amino-acid polymerization system, thereby locking in what would become the genetic code. Today, all organisms on earth share the same genetic code. Even though this genetic code arose through chance, the only differences in code units are partial differences in an extremely small number of species, thus implying that all organisms on earth are the descendants of a primitive life form that was born in a single random event.

Genome Imperialism

The primitive genetic information system was likely based on RNA. Although RNA carries genetic information, it can also function as a catalyst in the same manner as an enzyme. Therefore, scholars believe that RNA must have been more convenient than DNA for creating an initial fundamental system of life equipped with both informational and catalytic functions. However, RNA is far less stable than DNA, which may be why DNA was eventually established as the material for storing all of the genetic information in an organism (its genome) and why RNA became a vehicle for linking proteins and genes. These changes resulted in the mechanism for expressing genetic information that still exists today, in which DNA is transcribed into messenger RNA (mRNA), and the resulting mRNA sequence is translated into protein.

Before the total picture of genomic information was clear, the prevailing assumption was that the gene regions defining the structures of proteins in the genome were incredibly small. Ohno Susumu likened this conception to oases scattered across a desert. The idea was that most of the genome was barren. However, genome analysis continues to show us that a great deal of information is hidden in these supposedly barren areas. To be specific, some gene sequences have been found to produce RNA that is not translated into protein but instead involved in the regulation of gene expression and protein translation (microRNA). In addition, abnormalities in microRNAs trigger changes that can threaten the organism's life. Today, many researchers are frantically analyzing microRNA. MicroRNAs likely assemble partially with mRNA and partially with proteins. Through these associations, microRNAs are involved in the regulation of information essential to life. It is unlikely that this complex and sophisticated system was designed and built from the ground up.

The genetic information that forms the basis of life is abundant in chance, is limited, and lacks a syllogistic nature grounded in the principles of physics. Thus, the principles of life are defined by genomic information produced by laws unique to life—the basis of the concept of genome imperialism.

Mechanisms that Transcend the Limits of the Genome: Fluidity

From Finite to Infinite

In the previous section, I explained that the genome provides organisms with a limited framework, which is not only the fate of but also a defining characteristic of the mechanisms of life. What would happen if a limited existence remained in a particular state without ever changing at all? Humans, for example, would all have exactly the same faces. In reality, limited genomic information gives rise to individual organisms that are all different from one another, as well as to a wide variety of cells within a single organism. Thus, limited genomic information expresses presumably infinite diversity among all organisms. This level of qualitative amplification of information results from the synergy of many distinct mechanisms. However, as I described in the previous section, this amplification of information was not introduced by design but instead the result of the integration of diverse mechanisms that emerged fortuitously in a truly spectacular fashion.

First of all, individual humans, despite being of the same species, have vastly different genomes. These differences arose due to the accumulation of mutations in the genomes of individual organisms' germ cells during the process of evolution. These mutations are passed down to descendants and are distributed and expressed in the population as "polymorphisms," such as the four blood types (A, B, AB, and O) of the ABO blood group system. Polymorphisms and mutations are diverse, differing not only in genetic structure but also in number. In some cases, mutation leading to the partial deletion of gene function manifests in the form of genetic disease.

However, what is even more astonishing is that structural changes in the genome occur separately in the somatic cells that make up an individual organism. Thus, one of the keys that enables limited information to produce apparently infinite diversity is the dynamic fluidity of the information itself. Researchers have examined cases in which genetic information changes freely during an organism's life and expresses different functions in many different species.

The "Flexibility" of Changing Genes

One example of changes in genetic information is the genes that determine sex in yeast. In yeast, cell proliferation is regulated through conjugation according to an individual organism's recognition of sex. Yeast has two sex-determining genes: α and a. The expression of these two genes is modulated reversibly through "genetic recombination," the physical exchange of material between chromosomal loci of DNA.

As Figure 1a shows, the sex-determining genes α and a are inactive in their normal locations. When nutritional conditions or other circumstances require that yeast undergo zygotic division, either α or a is transported—via genetic recombination—to a chromosomal location where gene expression can occur (the mating-type locus [MAT]); as a result, one of the two sex-determining genes is expressed, thereby establishing the sex of the yeast organism as α or a. Yeast expressing the α gene secrete α factor and express a factor receptors. Conversely, yeast expressing the a gene secrete a factor and express α factor receptors. The binding of a factor or α factor to its receptor activates yeast, triggers the expression of multiple genes, and initiates conjugation (Figure 1b).

Flexibility in genetic information is also evident in the parasites called trypanosomes, which are transmitted by tsetse flies and cause sleeping sickness. By constantly switching antigenic substances (variant surface glycoprotein [VSG]) on their cell surfaces, trypanosomes evade their host's immune system and can proliferate until the host eventually loses its resistance. Among the thousand or so VSG archival or donor genes, partial conversion of even a part of a VSG gene changes its product, leading to the expression of VSG molecules that are so numerous and diverse as to be considered infinite.

As a contrast, let us look at acquired immunity, the most important biological defense mechanism in higher organisms. In acquired immunity, organisms with only limited genetic information recognize and remember a practically infinite number of antigens. This intriguing phenomenon has fascinated many biologists since the discovery of antibodies in the early twentieth century. In particular, as research further unraveled the structures of antibody molecules and those of the proteins' antigen-recognition sites, the question of how antibody genes can produce practically infinite and diverse antibodies aroused the curiosity of many a researcher.

Figure 1. Sex-determining gene recombination and mating in yeast

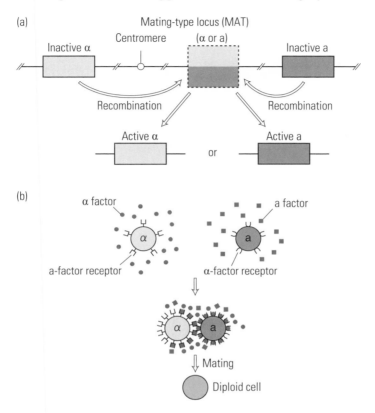

(a) In yeast, sex is determined via the transfer of the α gene or a gene to the mating-type locus (MAT). (b) Yeast expressing the α gene and yeast expressing the a gene release their respective factors, drawing the two yeast cells toward each other and leading to mating.

This riddle was solved in 1977 by Tonegawa Susumu, Leroy Hood, Philip Leder, and colleagues. What they found is that genetic information in antibody genes is rearranged as lymphocytes differentiate. This process of "gene rearrangement," through which fragments of genes are reorganized and joined together to produce new genes, occurs independently in individual lymphocytes. As a result, the immune system is able to express as many different antibody genes as there are lymphocytes in the body. For example, if there are 10 types of fragment A and 100 types of fragment B, and if the immune system were to produce a gene by randomly combining one type of both fragments, 1000 different genes would be produced. However, these 1000 different genes can be produced with just the base sequences necessary for slightly under 100 genes. The genes for the heavy chain and light chain that make up an antibody are rearranged via the recombination of three types and two types of fragments, respectively. The resulting information amplification is enormous, with a conservative estimate of a factor of 10^{10} (Figure 2).

As shown in Figure 2, each antibody is composed of four proteins—specifically two heavy chains and two light chains—that are linked together. Each heavy chain and light chain is divided into a variable domain and a constant domain. The variable domain, which is associated with antigen recognition, comprises three segments: variable (V), diversity (D; present in heavy chains only), and joining (J). Multiple gene fragments are pooled in the V, D, and J segments. One fragment is selected from each V, D, and J segment, and these three components are rearranged into the V gene exon. For example, a human heavy-chain gene contains 65 V gene segments, 27 D gene segments, and 6 J segments. These segments can be combined in 10,530 ways ($65 \times 27 \times 6$). As for human light-chain genes, there are two types: κ chains and λ chains. For κ chains, there are 40 V_κ segments and 5 J_κ segments. For λ chains, there are 30 V_λ segments and 4 J_λ segments. Therefore, light-chain gene segments can be combined in 320 ways ($40 \times 5 + 30 \times 4$). Furthermore, amino acids can be inserted or removed at each junction between segments, resulting in a diversity of at least 20 possible combinations at each junction. Adding all of the above numbers yields 2.7×10^{10} combinations of gene segments ($10,530 \times 320 \times 20 \times 20 \times 20$).

Consequently, the vast number of lymphocytes (10^{12}) throughout the human body comprise a repertoire in which nearly every lymphocyte expresses its own unique antigen receptor. Very few of these cells can react to a specific antigen to produce the corresponding antibody. However,

Figure 2. Antibody gene rearrangement

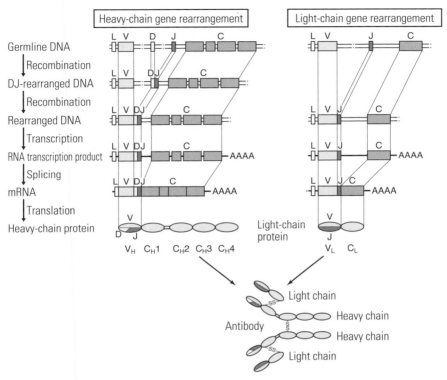

In the figure, rectangles represent exons; AAAA represents poly(A) tails added during transcription.

Reprinted with permission from Nishikawa, S. and Honjo, T., ed. 1999. *Men'eki to Ketsueki no Kagaku Iwanami Koza Gendai Igaku no Kiso 8* [The Science of Immunity and Blood, volume 8. Iwanami Courses: Principles of Current Medicine]. Iwanami Shoten.

when these few cells recognize an antigen, they proliferate and eventually differentiate into cells that produce antibodies in large quantities (see the section "Immune Memories Engraved into the Genome"). Some of the 10^{12} lymphocytes in the body do not react to any antigen, whereas others react to self antigens. However, the body is equipped with a mechanism that selectively kills or inactivates these harmful self-recognizing cells and then removes them. How surprising that the principle of Darwinian selection, which is based on chance mutations in genetic information and on an organism's environment, is applied as "survival of the fittest" among cells within an organism.

According to recent research into the ancestral forms of antibodies, jawless fish such as lampreys and hagfish possess primitive antibodies with a leucine-rich repeat structure. Although this ancestral molecule is a type of glycoprotein receptor with a completely different structure from that of an antibody molecule, it is nonetheless an antigen receptor formed through gene rearrangement.

Post-Transcriptional Editing of Genomic Information

As I explained earlier, the base sequence of the genome contains a portion that defines protein structures and a portion that does not. Moreover, the portion that defines protein structures is not a single continuous segment of genomic information. Instead, the information that makes up a gene is split into short segments called "exons" (primitive information units) that are distributed intermittently throughout the genome. The sequence between two exons is called an "intron," which is not directly associated with information. For example, the hemoglobin gene is divided into three segments. In the heavy-chain genes of antibodies, the variable region (V_H) and the constant region (C_H) are divided into two exons and four exons, respectively (see Figure 2). Furthermore, some genes contain even more exons; one example is the collagen gene, which is divided into 55 exons.

Why are genes split into exons? This is another question connected to the riddle of evolution. The most plausible theory today holds that when genetic information was first formed, it determined the structures of short, small protein units largely similar to exons, and various combinations and repetitions of these units gave rise to diverse genes. For example, the genes for alcohol dehydrogenase and lactate dehydrogenase contain exons corresponding to sites that recognize alcohol and lactate, respectively, as well as a separate common exon corresponding to the dehydrogenation-activity portion of the gene. The exon that codes for the dehydration reaction is highly similar between these two enzymes, suggesting that they both originated from a common ancestor. Most of the 55 exons of the collagen gene consist of 54 highly similar base pairs in which the sequence "glycine-amino acid X-amino acid Y" is repeated six times, corresponding to six units of the collagen helix. This demonstrates that the collagen gene emerged from the repetition of exons.

Translation of multiple exons into a protein that links the information in these exons requires a complex reaction called "splicing," in which the introns between exons are removed after they are transcribed to RNA, resulting in the formation of messenger RNA (mRNA). At the RNA stage, information is edited. In addition, different cells sometime splice the mRNA produced from the same gene into different combinations.

For example, at the terminus of the gene that produces an antibody heavy chain, there is an exon corresponding to the structure through which an antibody is embedded in the cell membrane. When this exon is expressed together with the rest of those in the gene, antibody molecules are expressed on the surfaces of B cells; these molecules can send an activation signal to other B cells after they have recognized an antigen. Thus, antibodies function as B-cell antigen receptors. In contrast, plasma cells (stimulated B cells that have matured to secrete large quantities of antibodies) do not need to recognize antigens and therefore produce mRNA that lack the exon encoding the membrane-embedding structure. As a result, antibody molecules are secreted outside plasma cells (and into serum) and capture antigens throughout the body. As this example shows, proteins made from the same gene can serve completely different physiological roles.

In another RNA editing mechanism, bases of genetic information in RNA transcripts are converted to produce proteins with completely different functions. A classic example of this phenomenon is an mRNA called ApoB100. This mRNA is translated as is in the liver to produce a transport protein for a type of cholesterol called "low-density lipoprotein." However, the RNA editing enzyme called APOBEC1 recognizes this mRNA and converts the C at a certain site to U, thereby changing what would be a glutamine residue (CAA) to a stop codon (UAA). This enzyme changes ApoB100 mRNA to ApoB48 mRNA, which produces a shorter protein (a chylomicron) that transports fatty acids (triglycerides) absorbed from the small intestine through the blood. Thus, this RNA editing mechanism assigns an important physiological function by changing just a single nucleotide.

mRNA editing is also necessary for the function of receptors related to central nervous system neurotransmitters, such as those for glutamate and serotonin. The editing of microRNAs, which I discussed earlier, has recently been found to change regulatory genes. The regulation of information is unfathomably complex.

The mechanism through which genes arise from exons is dynamic and fluid. The accumulation of genes gave rise to genomic information. The involvement of information editing, which uses the makeup of this genomic information to link segments of it in an ever-changing manner, flexibly adapts limited information to produce wide-ranging diversity. Thus, to use limited information in a nearly infinite fashion, organisms have mechanisms for applying that information dynamically and fluidly rather than strictly and stringently.

Mechanisms that Transcend the Limits of the Genome: Spatiotemporal Hierarchy

Astounding Diversity

Organisms are astoundingly diverse in their physical forms. For example, think of familiar insects and plants: they all have such unique forms that finding a consistent rule among them is a challenge. However, the 250-plus-year-old Linnaean system of classification, which is based on morphology, remains effective because form is a direct expression of organisms' diversity.

Diversity goes deeper than the level of individual organisms. Even a single organ demonstrates how shockingly diverse organisms are. One example is the eye, which is unique to a given species in terms of size and the shape of the lens. For example, the eyes of scallops do not have lenses but instead gather light with a concave mirror. Insects have compound eyes with thousands of small condenser lenses, enabling them to obtain visual information from a nearly 360° field of vision.

Darwin himself was keenly interested in the diversity of the eye among species and conducted detailed comparative studies on the topic. In *On the*

Origin of Species, he wrote, "To suppose that the eye [. . .] could have been formed by natural selection seems, I freely confess, absurd in the highest possible degree." However, recent molecular biological analysis has determined that the development of eyes, in all of their diverse forms, is regulated by the same genes (*Pax2* and *Pax6*). Although eyes in every species unmistakably underwent extensive evolution to achieve the optimal form for the environment in which that species arose, the fundamental fate-determining genes that produce visual organs have remained the same throughout the long process of evolution. What, then, is the mechanism that produces such astounding diversity on top of a common foundation?

The Hierarchical Nature of Information Expression

At the level of multicellular organisms, the number of genes in each species does not differ greatly, ranging from only 20,000 to 30,000. Despite this narrow range, genes produce astounding and diverse biologic forms, thanks to a hierarchical accumulation of information.

Unraveling the genomic program that constructs the forms of species is a central issue in embryology. In essence, an organism's form is generated through a program that determines what genes to activate at which sites in the embryo at which points in time after fertilization. In other words, the production of form depends on how the temporal and spatial axes of gene expression are regulated.

Of the 20,000 genes in humans, at least 1850 are transcription factors (genes involved in the regulation of gene expression). Furthermore, the regulation of a single gene involves not just one but four or five transcription factors. Therefore, combinations give rise to enormous diversity here as well. When you think about combinations of just four transcription factors among the thousands present in humans, the diversity of regulatory patterns is incredible. The main factor that produces the temporal axis is believed to be cascading hierarchical regulation, in which regulation of the expression of transcription factors themselves is regulated by other transcription factors. In other words, transcription factor A gives rise to factor B, which then gives rise to factor C.

The most crucial point in the production of form is the initiation of the spatial axis. A cell learns its position through adhering to nearby cells or signaling that takes place when signaling factors (such as growth-promoting factors) released from neighboring cells bind to receptors. One such example is cell-fate determination, in which a fertilized egg divides, forms an embryo, and then differentiates into endoderm (intestines, etc.), mesoderm (muscles, etc.), and ectoderm (nerves, etc.). This fate is determined by the concentration gradient of TGF family molecules (such as activin) secreted by the "organizer," a group of cells localized at a certain site in the embryo.

Both the temporal and spatial axes of gene expression are regulated via a hierarchy in which the birth of a molecule (or a cell) gives rise to a different molecule (or cell). For the spatial axis to be stabilized, cells must adhere to each other properly; if they do not, various organs cannot form. The liver, pancreas, and kidneys contain an incredible diversity of cells that are arranged systematically and form a specific structure. The factors involved in the adhesion of cells to each other come in two modes: one that involves the assembly of cells that express the same molecule on their surfaces and one in which different molecules come together like a key and a lock. The combination of these modes leads to the construction of astounding regularity and hierarchy.

The Hierarchical Nature of Signaling

The response of cells to external stimuli is simultaneously a basic mechanism of maintaining autonomy and self-replication in organisms, the latter of which is induced by a proliferative response. Cells respond to stimuli in three steps. In the first step, an external stimulant (such as a hormone, growth factor, differentiation factor, or bacterial substance) binds to a cell-surface receptor and changes its structure. In the second step, this structural change activates the receptor and the kinase (phosphorylating enzyme) bound to it, thereby triggering modifications (such as assembly and phosphorylation) of many molecules inside the cell, which in turn amplify signaling. Proteins not only function in their original forms but also undergo modifications, such as phosphorylation, that switch proteins on and off. At the same time, proteins also undergo functional regulation involving the hierarchy of a higher-order structure, in which phosphorylation promotes assembly with other proteins. For example, these modifications and regulatory mechanisms alter actin and microtubules, proteins that regulate cell shape, thereby causing the shape of cells to change.

In the third step of signaling, signals reach the nucleus of the cell and activate transcription factors. These factors induce the transcription of multiple genes, resulting in the production of new proteins in the cell. In summary, when a cell reacts to an external stimulus, a chain of multistep phosphorylation reactions exponentially activates the stimulus arising during a molecular aggregation reaction, causing major changes inside the cell and activating various molecules.

Hierarchy in Reverse

When we probe that signaling hierarchy, we run into two problems. First, in what order are genes hierarchically expressed to enable cells to differentiate? Conversely, in so-called "pluripotent cells," which possess the capacity to differentiate into all types of cells, which genes establish pluripotency? These are the inevitable questions we ponder when considering the process in reverse order—what forms cells take before they differentiate, what forms they take before that, and so on.

One major discovery that addresses these questions was announced by Professor Yamanaka Shinya and colleagues at the Institute for Frontier Life and Medical Sciences, Kyoto University. Dr. Yamanaka and associates learned that expressing four genes in mouse skin cells changed those cells into pluripotent stem cells (induced pluripotent stem cells [iPS cells]). Furthermore, by injecting these pluripotent cells into mouse embryos, they succeeded in generating mice in which the injected pluripotent cells had differentiated normally into various cell types throughout the body, including germline cells.

Dr. Yamanaka's group then succeeded in generating iPS cells from human cells as well. The ability to completely recover differentiation potential through only four genes greatly affected public policy regarding research on human embryonic stem cells in the United States. Previously, the prevailing assumption was that generating pluripotent stem cells would inevitably require harvesting cells from human embryos. However, the method devised by Dr. Yamanaka and colleagues enables the generation of pluripotent stem cells from a person's skin cells.

This major discovery has changed the course of regenerative medicine research, which prominent American investigators are already tackling in droves. As a result, the search for compounds that induce the dedifferentiation of differentiated cells into iPS cells and research on methods for inducing the differentiation of iPS cells into differentiated cells (such as blood cells) is progressing by leaps and bounds.

Although the diverse appearances of organisms and their common roots may seem contradictory at first glance, the involvement of the hierarchy of the temporal and spatial axes of genetic information provides an elegant explanation for that apparent contradiction. Furthermore, the pursuit of a fundamental question—"Are there genes that determine the pluripotency of embryonic cells?"—led to a discovery that has unexpectedly affected public policy on science and technology worldwide. This discovery drives home once again how important it is for researchers to take on fundamental problems.

Immune Memories Engraved into the Genome

Infections That Have Shaped History

The greatest contribution that medical research has made to humanity is the prevention of infections through vaccines. How do vaccines prevent infections? Their power stems from the memories present in the immune system. When the immune system encounters an antigen that it has encountered before, it can mount an immune response more rapidly, powerfully, and effectively the second time around. Therefore, if a person who has already been infected with a weakly virulent pathogen later encounters a highly virulent strain of the same pathogen, strong immunity can minimize the infection symptoms.

Vaccines are said to have originated in 1796, when the English physician Edward Jenner developed a vaccine for smallpox. However, humanity has known for thousands of years that sometimes a person who has narrowly escaped death from an infection never develops the same disease again.

During a battle between Carthage and a Sicilian colonial city in 405 BCE, a plague erupted on the front lines, ravaging both armies and forcing the

Carthaginians to retreat. In 397 BCE, the Carthaginians formed a new military and attacked Sicily again, but a plague once again broke out on the front lines. The Sicilian army consisted primarily of soldiers who had survived the plague eight years earlier; therefore, very few of them fell ill again, and those who did fall ill had only mild symptoms. In contrast, the newly formed Carthaginian army saw many of its troops fall ill and suffered a massive defeat.

Infections have shaped human history time and again since then. The Black Death that struck Europe during the Middle Ages is said to have killed half of the population of England in the fifteenth century. However, some of the monks and nuns who fell ill while nursing patients reportedly later recovered and never again got sick from the Black Death even as it raged on.

Based on the premise that experiencing an infection leads to immunity, Dr. Jenner conceived of a smallpox vaccine. As a result, humanity ultimately achieved the triumph of eradicating smallpox worldwide in 1980.

The Evolution of the Immune System

The immune system is a necessary mechanism for the survival of an organism. Prior to the development of medical science, infections were often fatal. Evolutionarily, the genetic information for defending against infections goes all the way back to insects. However, the immunity in insects is so-called innate immunity; there has never been any evidence of immune memory in insects.

Innate immunity uses receptors to recognize shared patterns in the structures of pathogens and elicits a response in the organism to those pathogens. Targets of recognition include substances that make up the membrane of a pathogen and nucleic acid structures unique to pathogens. The receptors that recognize patterns in innate immunity are called Toll receptors and were first discovered in insects. Actually, Toll receptors play two roles, as they were initially discovered as a differentiation regulation receptor necessary for development in insects. A similar mechanism (innate immunity) was later determined to exist in vertebrates as well, with receptors called Toll-like receptors (TLRs). In humans, 11 TLRs have been discovered to date. These TLRs are expressed primarily on macrophages and activate an organism's immune system by reacting to a pathogen's membrane or nucleic acids. However, further research is necessary to determine the importance of TLRs in humans.

Vertebrate organisms possess a defense system that expands rapidly: acquired immunity. This incredibly advanced defense system not only recognizes antigens individually and specifically but also memorizes them. For the immune system to recognize antigens specifically, lymphocytes must express diverse antigen receptors, corresponding to each individual antigen. Antigen receptors take on an incredible variety of forms during the process of lymphocyte differentiation and are expressed in their completed forms on the surfaces of mature lymphocytes. Each individual lymphocyte expresses a single antigen receptor.

As I described earlier in this chapter, this expression of diverse antigen receptors is the product of antibody gene rearrangement in lymphocytes, which shatters the limits of genomic information.

The Memory of the Immune System

Antibodies are antigen receptors produced by B cells and secreted into the blood. Antibodies produced during the developmental process are collectively called "natural antibodies," which form an individual's antibody repertoire. The discovery of vaccines at the end of the eighteenth century enabled Emil von Behring and Kitasato Shibasaburo to realize at the end of the nineteenth century that substances that recognize and neutralize (deactivate) antigens are present in blood. Subsequent progress in the chemical analysis of antigen-recognizing substances has demonstrated, as is understood currently, that antibodies have a "variable region" that binds to antigens and a "constant region" that processes bound antigens by various means. When an antigen (pathogen) invades an organism, a B cell recognizes the antigen due to the antigen receptor on the B cell's surface, reacts powerfully, and proliferates dramatically. During this process, B cells change the structures of antibody molecules and thus remember antigens.

There are two mechanisms by which antibody molecules remember antigens: somatic hypermutation and class switching. In somatic hypermutation, a point mutation is introduced into the variable region of an antibody gene in a B cell, changing the amino-acid sequence of the antibody produced to have an enhanced capacity to bind antigen. These point mutations in antibody genes occur at random. Most antibodies that arise through random mutation are not suited to binding antigens. However, in incredibly rare but sufficiently frequent cases, a B cell will possess a gene that produces antibodies with dramatically enhanced capacity for binding an antigen. Antigenic stimulation of such cells (the binding of an antigen to its receptor, or antibody, on the cell's surface) induces them to proliferate rapidly. These cells then become long-lived immune cells (memory B cells) that maintain antibody memories.

Darwinian principles work effectively yet again in this process. Specifically, among the cells with genes that have undergone random mutations, only those cells that bind antigens powerfully increase their descendants. The establishment of this population of cells is what produces immunological memory.

The other mechanism for remembering antigens is class switching. As B cells differentiate, the first antibody (or antigen receptor) to appear is the IgM class. Antigen stimulation then yields the antibody classes IgG, IgE, and IgA, which differ in their antigen-processing capacities. The class of an antibody is determined by the constant region of its heavy chain. After an antibody binds an antigen, different actions, such as antigen processing (degradation and phagocytosis) and mobilization of other inflammatory cells, occur depending on the class. For example, antibodies of the IgA class are readily secreted from mucous membranes. Antibody class is changed through the genetic modification mechanism called class-switch recombination, in which the constant region gene is changed. This switch remains as an antibody memory. As a result, when an antigen is encountered again, the class best suited to process that antigen can be produced immediately.

Antibody memories thus form through the phenomena of somatic hypermutation, which introduces mutation into the variable region of an antibody gene, and class switching, where the class determined by an antibody gene's constant region changes. Both of these phenomena involve genetic modification. To put it the other way around, antibody memories remain because they are engraved into antibody genes (Figure 3).

Figure 3. AID engraves antibody memories

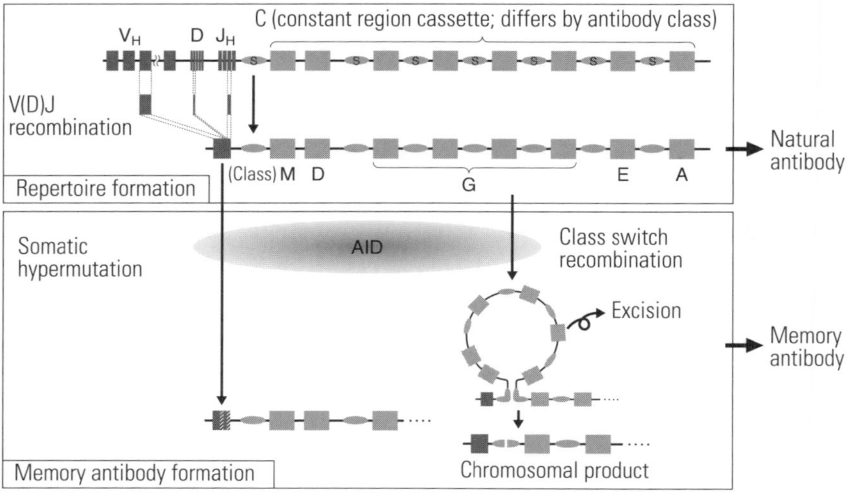

AID: The Key to Antibody Memories

By the 1970s, the scientific community had a detailed understanding of antibody molecules. In the subsequent 30 years, somatic hypermutation was definitively proven to result from point mutation in a gene, and the mechanism behind gene rearrangement in class switching was determined. However, there was one more major riddle: what engraves antibody memories into the genome?

In 2000, our research group determined that an enzyme called AID (activation-induced cytidine deaminase) is responsible for engraving these mutations into the genome (Figure 3). In addition to determining that AID is necessary for both somatic hypermutation and class switching, we learned the surprising fact that—when present—AID can always trigger these reactions. To be specific, antibody memories induced by vaccines are engraved into the genomes of B cells when the expression of AID is induced by B-cell activation. All vertebrates with acquired immunity possess AID. However, we are still left with the issue of how AID introduces mutations into the genome.

Antibody memories form through two phenomena: somatic hypermutation, which introduces a mutation into the variable region of an antibody gene; and class switching, in which the class of an antibody gene's constant region is changed. Both of these phenomena involve genetic modification.

Meanwhile, a shocking development occurred in 2006: in addition to its primary role as the engraver of immune memory in antibody genes, AID was implicated in cancer through the enzyme's ability to introduce mutations in cancer genes when it was expressed in cells other than lymphocytes due to their infection by pathogens. Expression of AID has been reported in liver cells infected with the hepatitis C virus and in parietal cells (cells in the stomach wall) infected with *Helicobacter pylori*. AID has also been determined to play an important role in Burkitt's lymphoma in humans and in mouse plasmacytoma, a similar cancer.

Assuming that these findings are accurate, they show that in addition to its role in protecting the self, AID has also been burdened with the unfortunate role of triggering cancerous transformation. It is truly ironic that AID, which is responsible for engraving immune memories into the genome, should also play a part in the onset of cancer. The most important thing for any organism is to reproduce and leave descendants. When you compare dying from an infection before reaching reproductive age to dying from a tumor in old age, it is of course more important to avoid dying from infection, even when considering the danger posed by cancer. However, AID may have a greater role that has not yet been revealed.

Inner Infinity: The Ever-Growing Number of Species

Too Many Species to Describe Them All

Just how many species are there on earth? This question is impossible to answer accurately because there is no comprehensive list of all species on earth. Various estimates abound; even just the number of confirmed species is roughly 1.8 million, and some estimates hold that another 10 million species have yet to be confirmed. Despite humanity having unceasingly described new species in the 200-plus years since the introduction of the

Linnaean system for classifying and describing species, the number of described species continues to grow constantly. Curious species of turtles and fish that emerge above ground only when it rains have been discovered in an equatorial desert in Brazil. New insect species are also sometimes reported. Even Emperor Akihito described several new species of fish.

Bacteria species have recently been determined to be unimaginably diverse. In the past, classification of bacteria consisted of culturing them and then describing the organisms that grew based on the properties of their forms and metabolic pathways. Although subsequent research made it possible to identify bacteria by sequencing them, there was no way to describe species that could not be cultured.

However, it later became possible to determine the genetic sequence of bacteria by amplifying their DNA without culturing them; this led to the birth of the new field called "metagenomics." Metagenomics is based on the method that was used to sequence the human genome. First, DNA is extracted from several bacterial cells and randomly fragmented, and these fragments are then sequenced. Next, through the power of information technology, the sequences of these fragments are linked by using the partial overlaps between them. This linking of fragments yields the entire DNA sequence of a single species of bacteria. With this method, it is possible to sequence the genetic information of bacteria living in the deep sea or thousands of meters underground without culturing them or even being able to observe their forms within the material in which they exist.

The Great Latent Power of Bacteria

The metagenomic discovery of new bacteria has raised hopes that they may have unexpected useful applications. The relationship between microbes and humans dates far back to the fermentation of substances such as alcohol and miso. The culture of useful bacteria has brought tremendous benefits to humanity. More recently, the great power of microbes has been harnessed to produce antibiotics and synthesize vitamins. In the last few years, microbes have been applied in sewage treatment technology, an area drawing attention for its role in environmental protection; however, the microorganisms actually at work here have not yet been determined. Isolating and making further artificial improvements to the microorganisms with powerful environmental purification capacity will likely contribute toward solutions to global environmental problems.

Bacteria allow for even bigger dreams. For example, microbes that grow deep in the sea or in other unique environments are expected to have as-yet-unknown possibilities. The field of study that concentrates on these microbes (green chemical engineering) offers potential for major developments, such as the production of energy resources like ethanol and butanol from biological waste products and the generation of primary chemical engineering products like ethylene via reduction of those energy resources.

In addition to this practical aspect, the fact that deep-sea microbes are able to survive in the high heat and pressure around hydrothermal vents suggests that these organisms live in the conditions on earth that are closest to those present at the dawn of life. Many life scientists anticipate that analysis of these microbes may provide clues to the origins of life.

The Benefits of Symbiotic Bacteria

Many types of microorganisms dwell within our bodies and those of other animals. Many of these microbes have a symbiotic (mutually beneficial) relationship with their hosts. A particularly famous example in plants is the symbiosis between legumes and the bacteria called "rhizobia." Thanks to the nitrogen components that rhizobia produce, legumes do not require nitrogen-containing fertilizer. At the same time, rhizobia get their energy from the photosynthesis products of legumes. Countless symbiotic bacteria live in the guts of humans, insects, and various other animals.

In humans, gut bacteria play many crucial roles such as providing their hosts with vitamins and aiding the degradation and metabolism of food. Meanwhile, the host provides gut bacteria with a constant environment that gives them access to a stable energy source, thus helping the bacteria reproduce.

Gut bacteria in humans and mice have been determined to have an absolutely crucial interdependence with the immune system. Animals raised in sterile environments have insufficiently developed immune systems, as evidenced by the shrinking of lymph nodes in Peyer's patches and elsewhere in the gut. Thus, a symbiotic relationship exists in which the presence of gut bacteria provides constant immune stimulation from bacterial components, enabling the development of the immune system throughout the body.

The human gut contains more than 100 trillion microbes (compared with 60 trillion total cells in the human body) consisting of hundreds of species. Although some of these bacteria, such as lactobacilli (lactic acid bacteria), aid in the metabolism of food, others such as the anaerobic bacteria called clostridia harm the body when they overgrow. In immunodeficient humans and mice unable to produce IgA, anaerobic bacteria overgrow, causing the immune system to overreact. As this example shows, gut bacteria preserve a constant balance based on interaction with their host via the immune system. In other words, we live in symbiosis with large numbers of organisms living inside our bodies through a give-and-take relationship.

The Effect of Symbiotic Bacteria on Evolution

Research on symbiotic bacteria has also given rise to new developments in evolutionary thought. These developments are ignited by the finding that bacteria exchange genes with each other quite frequently.

An idea that is widely accepted today holds that eons ago in the history of evolution, bacteria infiltrated the cells of the ancestors of eukaryotes and established themselves there. We can see vestiges of this infiltration in the forms of the mitochondria in eukaryotic cells and the chloroplasts in plant cells. Analysis of mitochondrial DNA and chloroplast DNA has revealed the undisputable fact that these gene clusters originate from ancient bacteria. This finding demonstrates an extreme form of symbiosis. Mitochondria and chloroplasts, which are collectively called organelles, contain unique genetic information (DNA) completely different from that of the cell nucleus. This genetic information is also copied in synchrony with cell division and handed down to new organelles. Due to their role as the generators of energy in a cell, mitochondria are indispensable. In fact, abnormalities in mitochondrial genes are known to cause various diseases.

Symbiosis inside cells means that bacteria lose their independence as organisms and that their fates are tied to those of the host cells. However, although part of the information of those bacteria remains within the organism, some of it is presumed to have transferred into the DNA of the host cells.

DNA Exchange Produces New Species

Genomic information is routinely exchanged through chromosomal crossover and chiasma formation (the point of physical contact between chromosome copies) during sexual reproduction. In addition, microbes have sexes and have long been known to exchange genetic information via conjugation. Once an antimicrobial-resistance gene, for example, gets on the same plasmid (a genetic factor that proliferates and is passed down to descendants independently of chromosomes) as sex-determining factors, it spreads immediately to other microbes of the same species.

Meanwhile, research on marine microbes has shown that different species of bacteria share several remarkably similar series of gene clusters that include photoreceptor proteins (rhodopsin) and the retinal biosynthesis pathway. This finding suggests that gene clusters are exchanged within populations of microbes according to some undetermined mechanism. If this exchange were highly frequent, new species would be born more often than is currently assumed. In the gut, high-temperature seawater, and other semi-closed environments with high densities of organisms, genomic information could be exchanged between individuals of different species more frequently than previously predicted.

Research in this field is still nascent. However, assuming that exchanges of genetic information frequently generate new species one after another within the biological system on Earth, the number of species on our planet would truly be infinite.

Birth, Aging, Illness, Death

The Death of Cells and the Death of the Individual

Everything that lives must die. This is the great law of life. However, this law applies specifically to organisms as individuals. In prokaryotes such as *E. coli*, the individual organism and germ cells are nearly identical, meaning that their lives are continuous due to repeated cell division. Consequently, prokaryotes are not considered to have "lifespans." Therefore, the concept of lifespans began with the dawn of sexual reproduction between multicellular organisms, when the continuity of the germ cells that link generations was dissociated from the death of the individual.

Although the death of an organism is the death of an individual, the death of cells within an individual is an everyday occurrence. A form of cell death called "apoptosis" occurs frequently to maintain function in an organism by means such as involvement in morphogenesis during development and the elimination of self-recognizing lymphocytes in the immune system.

No one knows why individuals have lifespans. However, the lifespan of an organism is undoubtedly programmed within its genetic information. The basic characteristics of organisms are self-renewal, adaptability, and autonomy. An individual's lifespan is likely determined by a finiteness hidden in one of these three major basic mechanisms of functional maintenance.

The Genes that Determine Lifespan

The search for the genes that determine lifespan has come alive in recent years. Studies using fruit flies and nematodes (roundworms) indicate that multiple genes are associated with lifespan. However, science has not yet pieced together the full picture of the program that determines lifespan. According to one theory, each cell is assigned a set number of divisions and dies once it exceeds this set number; these cell deaths are held to be associated with the overall lifespan of the individual. Experimental data from cultured cells show that cells undergo a specified number of divisions due to the shortening of telomeres (structures at the ends of every chromosome) that occurs with each cell division; this finding supports the theory that cells themselves have a set lifespan program.

However, not all cells divide repeatedly. Considering the presence of stem cells, many today believe it is unlikely that lifespan can be explained by the number of cell divisions alone. Another theory holds that lifespan is determined by the accumulation of toxic substances due to oxidative stress (the body's inability to counteract toxic intracellular substances), and yet another theory posits that lifespan ends due to the accumulation of genetic mutations resulting from radiation.

Genetic research on nematodes has identified genes that affect lifespan via several point mutations, a finding that gives great hope to researchers attempting to understand lifespan at the molecular level. However, I personally find it inconceivable that lifespan would be determined by such a miniscule number of genes. As I stated earlier, I believe that a mechanism with hidden finiteness is incorporated into the basic mechanisms of self-renewal, adaptability, and autonomy.

When the media went crazy over iPS cells, some people seemed to have the idea that by replacing individual organs over and over with new ones, humans could perhaps live forever. However, iPS cells most likely will not bring about eternal life. In addition, considering the history and characteristics of organisms, eternal life is not something we should strive for. To give a specific example, replacing an individual's brain is quite impossible. I believe that life is significant because we die.

Struggling against the Environment: Adaptation Determines Survival

Significant emphasis is placed on the fact that genetic information achieves two goals that seem mutually contradictory at a glance: to adapt well to the environment, and to escape from environmental factors and preserve a certain level of autonomy. That is, genetic information must be equipped with all of the programs necessary for an organism to survive in the environment in which it has been placed. To put that the other way around, the organisms and groups of those organisms that were able to construct those programs are the ones that have survived. Therefore, an organism's survival is established through the balance of the tension and harmony between inborn information (genetic information) and acquired information (environmental factors).

The immune system is a magnificent example of this balance. Higher organisms possess an astounding capacity to defend against infections by adapting to their environments. Specifically, higher organisms possess a mechanism that enables them to resist unknown pathogens by modifying the structures of their antigen-recognition genes. In vertebrates, genomic information contains a flexible mechanism that enables the immune system to adapt to nearly any pathogen; this mechanism has undoubtedly conferred vertebrates with remarkably extended lifespans. This mechanism is particularly notable in B cells, where the structures of pathogens (environmental information) are engraved as mutations into the genes of the antibodies that recognize those structures, enabling B cells to produce memory antibodies.

Food quality, another environmental factor, also results in epigenetic changes (in which gene sequences themselves do not change but gene expression changes due to changes in modification), although these changes are not as dramatic as those described earlier. In an experiment from long ago, high-calorie diets shortened the lifespans of rats. Genetic research on nematodes has demonstrated two findings related to lifespan. The first of these is that undernutrition leads to longer lifespans than overnutrition. The second finding is that lifespan is extended through mutations in insulin-like growth-factor receptors (IGFRs), which are associated with nutrient intake, and by mutations in the IGFR signaling pathway. According to one study in mice, partial removal of the signals from insulin receptors extended lifespan by 18%. In mammals, growth hormone and IGF1 signals have been said to be involved in lifespan.

Although data from nematodes cannot be applied directly to humans, the quality of food is known to trigger changes in gene expression in humans as well. Many high-profile metabolic diseases such as diabetes, hyperlipidemia, and hypertension have been demonstrated to be greatly affected by the balance between calorie intake and calorie expenditure. Environmental information in the form of epigenetic changes is believed to trigger semi-irreversible changes in gene expression systems. As the example of metabolic diseases shows, genetic information and environmental information share strong associations with each other, and a shift in the balance between them triggers a shift into a pathologic state.

Diseases in the Gap between Environment and Genes

So, what sort of state is disease? One could argue that disease includes any state of defectiveness in the function of an organism in the environment in which it has been placed. This state is affected by two broad factors.

The first possibility is that some mutation in genetic information, the fundamental information of organisms, renders the body incapable of executing biological functions smoothly, a state referred to as "congenital disease" (present at birth). The other possibility is a state in which biological functions are maintained with no problems whatsoever in a normal environment but are rendered insufficient when environmental factors change. A typical example of this state is infection. Of course, diseases caused by insufficient nutrient intake can be considered examples of this state as well.

In reality, most diseases occur due to a combination of environmental and genetic factors. To put it another way, disease is a state in which a mismatch occurs between congenital genetic information and information acquired due to environmental factors.

Infections, previously thought to be caused almost completely by environmental factors, are being increasingly understood to be determined by genetic factors as well. For example, researchers have determined that leprosy, which people believed for many years to be incurable, occurs when abnormalities in genes related to the immune system make the body susceptible to infection by *Mycobacterium leprae*. This situation resembles influenza viruses in that, despite encountering the same virus, some people become severely ill while others suffer only mild symptoms.

Another example of infection, the AIDS virus (HIV), comprises a mere 15 genes. This virus proliferates by hijacking multiple genes from its host, after which disease ultimately manifests. People with and without resistance to HIV are known to demonstrate differences in several genes. The addition of genetic factors on top of the weight of environmental factors has enormous effects on the onset of disease.

Individual differences in HIV resistance can be explained by a mutation in the CCR5 gene, which was selected for study because it was found in people who encountered and survived bubonic plague. Other similar examples are malaria and sickle cell disease, which I briefly discussed earlier. Basically, the genetic information we carry today is the accumulation of information selected by past environmental factors.

The same is true of metabolic diseases. Just after the birth of *Homo sapiens* around 200,000 years ago, the environment clearly did not offer enough food; keeping blood glucose at or above a certain level was essential for survival. The circumstances of our current world, in which people can actually overeat, run wholly counter to the genetic information that existed when modern humans emerged evolutionarily. As a result, our genetic information is not necessarily sufficiently equipped to handle abnormally high blood glucose or lipid levels. Consequently, obesity, diabetes, hypercholesterolemia, hypertension, and various other metabolic diseases have become a major problem not only in developed countries but everywhere around the world.

These examples clearly illustrate that disease occurs due to a mismatch between environmental factors and inborn information.

The Mission of Medical Science

The purpose of medical science is to release humanity from the grip of disease, not so that we might live forever but so that we may live to our appointed times. As I have already explained, human lifespans are greatly affected by environmental factors. Thanks to improvements in nutrition and hygiene, the average lifespan is double what it was 200 years ago, at least in developed countries. However, life is life because it is finite and will likely never go on forever. In this regard, understanding the mechanism that programs lifespan is a crucial area of research that touches on the origin of life.

Clearly the mission of medical science is to cure disease in order to help patients achieve contentment (happiness). However, as I explained at the beginning of this chapter, human happiness does not reach a higher level until its other factor—the elimination of anxiety—is fulfilled.

Because they face death, the greatest source of anxiety, the sick unsurprisingly fall into a state of anxiety. Saving people from this state was long the role of religion. Birth, aging, illness, and death are the four universal sufferings preached by the Buddha. However, our current society has been constructed in such a way that all four of these sufferings are in the hands of physicians. These doctors need to realize that their role is no longer merely to cure illness but that they also need to assume part of the role of a religious figure. The mission of physicians today is not only to devote themselves to curing disease but also to eliminate their patients' anxiety and enable them to taste true happiness. However, patients must understand that their doctors' capabilities and roles are limited. I hear that more and more patients over-rely on doctors and take it for granted that their illnesses will be cured. However, this is a gravely mistaken assumption. Patients must understand that much of medical science is about helping them to heal on their own.

The patient's power to live as an organism is the foundation of their power to fight illness. People cannot run from birth, aging, illness, or death. Instead, we must all go through life bearing these burdens and, hopefully, live until our appointed times. The Buddha's insight is alive in the way we think about life today.

Cancer: An Agonizing Conflict between Cells and the Individual

Cancer Is a Genetic Disease

Of the diseases that beset humanity, none affects as many people's ways of life as cancer. Although death awaits us all, many people simply hope not to get cancer. Obviously, cancer is a phenomenon that occurs only in multicellular organisms. The tragedy of cancer is that some of the body's cells deviate from the overall regulation of the organism and proliferate endlessly, thereby bringing about the death of the individual. Thus, patients with cancer have to await death while trapped in a cruel paradox: the proliferation of cells that were originally part of the body leads to the death of the individual.

In 1971, the United States government launched "The War on Cancer," an endeavor on the order of the Apollo Project to put humans on the moon. Under the leadership of President Nixon, the cancer project became law. To start with, the US government granted an eye-popping additional USD100 million in research funds to the National Institutes of Health. But in 1993, the members of a review panel expressed their disappointment regarding the little overall progress against cancer—compared with the considerable developments in molecular biology and basic research—despite the billions of research dollars allocated to the NCI since 1971. The most noteworthy finding generated through those enormous funds was that cancer is a genetic disease. However, numerous and incredibly diverse mutations are involved in different types of cancer. In addition, cancer is likely caused not by a mutation in a single gene but by mutations in multiple genes. To be specific, these include mutations in genes involved in the regulation of cell proliferation and the cell cycle, genes for transmitters that send proliferation signals to cells, genes related to regulation of transcription of genes involved in proliferation, and genes involved in DNA repair—a truly diverse range of gene mutations.

Since the previous century, various environmental factors called "mutagens," such as coal tar, which was proven to be a mutagen by Professor Yamagiwa Katsusaburo, have been known to ultimately injure genes and thereby trigger cancer. Similarly, in cancers triggered by viruses, the viruses cause abnormal expression or mutations of genes involved in growth regulation, resulting in cancerous transformation.

Thus, compared with where we were 40 years ago, great strides have been made in unraveling the causes of cancer.

Proto-Oncogenes and Tumor Suppressor Genes

Some cancers referred to as "familial cancers" have been shown to depend on genetic background. A classic example is retinoblastoma, in which mutation in the RB1 gene (involved in cell-cycle regulation) triggers congenital cancer of the retina. Each child has a pair of RB1 genes and inherits one copy from each parent. However, retinoblastoma does not develop immediately after a single mutation in one gene copy but instead develops only after another mutation occurs in the second copy of the RB1 gene at some time after birth. Thus, a child who inherits a mutated RB1 gene from one parent will develop retinoblastoma after just one mutation in the gene copy from the other parent, meaning that the probability of developing cancer congenitally is incredibly high. Curiously, although the RB1 gene should function in all types of cells throughout the body, cancer manifests only in the retina.

Genes such as RB1 that cause cancer only when mutations occur in both gene copies inherited from both parents are called "tumor suppressor genes." Because tumor suppressor genes negatively regulate cell proliferation, cells continue to proliferate normally as long as one of the two genes is normal. In contrast, cancer can also develop when cell proliferation is dramatically accelerated due to a point mutation in only one gene copy of a pair. One example is the genes for proteins called Ras, which transmit proliferative stimuli into cells. Thus, a mutation in just one of a pair of genes can trigger cancer; these types of genes are called "proto-oncogenes" (genes that lead to cancer).

The Risk of Oncogenesis Is Woven into the Genome

Earlier, I discussed the AID gene, which introduces mutations into genes to boost antibody gene diversity and memory of foreign enemies. Expression of AID normally occurs only in B cells and is subject to close regulation. However, viral infections have been demonstrated to cause abnormal expression of AID in cells other than B cells. This abnormal expression of AID is in the spotlight for its potential connection to oncogenesis (the development of cancer).

If AID is expressed abnormally, unexpected mutations will be introduced into cells other than B cells, potentially mutating oncogenes (cancer genes) and tumor suppressor genes. In other words, defense genes that bypass the limits of the genome can actually cause cancer.

How Far Have Anti-Cancer Drugs Come?

Despite the efforts made in the ambitious War on Cancer, science has unfortunately discovered almost no revolutionary wonder drugs to treat cancer. Although cancer research has indeed made a world of difference in the diagnosis and prognoses of cancer since 1971, these results are largely attributable to advances in methods of diagnosis and prevention. One reason for the lack of progress in discovering a wonder drug for cancer is that the genes that trigger cancer are incredibly diverse. Most cancer researchers believe that discovering a drug that would work on all types of cancer likely is almost impossible.

The most rudimentary treatment for cancer is the use of drugs to stop the proliferation of cells. However, this method stops the proliferation of normal cells as well, resulting in major side effects that cause patients great suffering. New compounds that inhibit cell proliferation are constantly emerging. Although these newer compounds inflict milder side effects and are more effective than early compounds, every anticancer drug designed to

Figure 4. Imatinib: A Leukemia Drug Born of Tertiary Structural Analysis

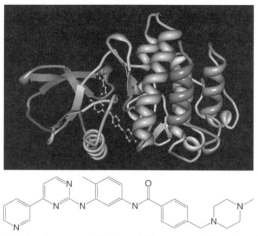

(a) Imatinib bound to its target, Abl kinase (b) The structural formula of imatinib

This figure is reprinted with permission from Cowan-Jacob, S.W. et al. 2007. "Structural Biology Contributions to the Discovery of Drugs to Treat Chronic Myelogenous Leukemia." *Acta Crystallographica Section D* 63: 80–93.

inhibit cell proliferation causes some side effects. Current research on this type of anticancer drug is focused on drug delivery—how to design these drugs so they are taken up only by specific targets (cancer cells).

The best anticancer drug developed in recent years is imatinib, which specifically inhibits a type of kinase (Bcr-Abl tyrosine kinase) that transmits signals for leukocyte (white blood cell) growth factors. This kinase is specifically expressed only by leukocytes that have undergone chromosomal translocation. Structural analysis of this kinase led to the chemical structure of imatinib, which is why imatinib is so highly specific and incredibly effective. The three-dimensional molecular structural analysis that produced imatinib also led to the development of dasatinib, a treatment for imatinib-resistant leukemia. Dasatinib and imatinib (Figure 4) are excellent examples of basic medical research leading directly to treatment. As a result, many patients with leukemia now survive much longer after developing their disease than they used to.

The Development of Cancer Immunotherapy

Cancer immunotherapy has recently been in the spotlight as a new treatment for cancer. However, cancer immunotherapy is not at all a novel idea. Since long ago, some researchers have believed that cancer is a foreign entity to the body and that the immune system may be able to eliminate it. Early attempts at cancer immunotherapy included studies that focused on highly malignant skin cancers like melanoma, in which melanocytes (melanin-producing cells) become cancerous. This study searched aggressively for immunogens (substances that induce an immune response) among the proteins expressed by melanocytes and identified several powerful immunostimulatory peptides (relatively short amino acids that activate the immune system). These peptides were somewhat successful in modulating cancer in animals. However, the application of these peptides to cancer in humans did not yield the expected results. A different attempt at cancer immunotherapy involved taking cells associated with the innate immune system (which are less specific in their anti-invader activity than cells from the acquired immune system), activating them in test tubes, and reinfusing them into the donor body to overcome cancer. However, this attempt also failed to produce the anticipated results.

Later, a new way of thinking about cancer immunotherapy emerged. In the early stage after cancer develops, the body is exposed for a long time to large quantities of distinctive antigens expressed by cancer cells. Immunologically speaking, this is a state in which antigen excess is likely to trigger immune tolerance. In a state of immune tolerance, antigen excess prevents effective activation of the immune system. In that case, how can cancer immunotherapy be made to work? The key is to reactivate the immune system by deactivating the mechanism that triggers immune tolerance.

Recent research has demonstrated that both activation signals and deactivation signals are involved in the immune system and that a balance between the two types of signals is what enables immune responses to function properly. This means that once the immune system is activated, it must be moderately suppressed, or side effects from excess activation such as inflammation will inevitably occur. To use a car as an analogy, the immune system is only able to serve its role properly as a defense system once it is equipped with both an accelerator and a brake.

Immune tolerance is like a car in which the brake on immune response is stuck to the floor. The idea of releasing this brake is what finally propelled cancer immunotherapy into clinical trials.

The Feat of Living

If you consider that point mutations occur at a certain frequency in humans' genetic information, the emergence of cancer cells is inevitable. Cancer cells do not pose a problem as long as they do not grow so large that their continued division interferes with the functioning of the individual. If cancer cells are recognized and eliminated by the immune system at an early stage, they will disappear before the individual experiences any subjective symptoms. However, immune function eventually declines with age. The longer someone lives, the more likely it is that cancer cells will manifest. Thus, the manifestation of cancer cells itself partially determines our lifespans.

The three factors of life are self-renewal, autonomy, and adaptability; cancer is essentially the manifestation of cells that critically lack adaptability. Cancer cells autonomously acquire energy and proliferate endlessly. If a single cell within the environment of an individual organism deviates from regulation in that environment and continues to proliferate, that environment will collapse. Cancer, basically a conflict between cells and the individual over self-replication, forces us to think about the fundamental fate of life.

The Long Road to Understanding the Mind

The Mind Is a Function of the Brain

René Descartes said, "I think; therefore, I am." In the same vein, questions of the mind such as, "What am I?" and "What makes me 'me'?" are concerns not just for philosophers but also for all humanity.

I doubt anyone would object to the claim that the mind is a function of the brain. As organisms evolved, the function of the brain evolved to an advanced level. The first central nervous system was likely sensory organs. Mechanisms that detect external information and link it to action are evident even in single-celled organisms such as bacteria, which move by sensing light, and amoebas, which move towards food. The brains of insects have the capacity to learn and remember where flower nectar is and inform other members of its species. Although the genomes of humans and chimpanzees are considered to be more than 98% identical, the volume of the human brain is nearly double that of the chimpanzee brain, suggesting that human brain function is incredibly advanced. In particular, the human brain is considered to be characterized by its dramatically expanded frontal lobe, the region responsible for integrating the functions of other lobes, in comparison to that in chimpanzees.

The mind has two main types of function: rational activity, which consists of judgment, cognition, and comprehension, and sensitivity, which consists primarily of emotion. Memory straddles both of these categories. The mind is difficult to research because it is difficult to measure directly. In animal studies, what can actually be measured are actions that manifest as integrations of rationality, sensitivity, memory, and so on. These measurable actions are then used as a basis to infer the mechanisms of each of these basic capabilities.

Generating genetically modified mice with reversible knockout of specific molecules in specific locations or at desired times has been a spectacularly successful method for measuring behavioral abnormalities and abnormal reactions in animals. However, there is quite a bit of distance between actions and the mind.

What Brain Damage Has Taught Us

The greatest contributions of brain research have perhaps come from clinical analyses of patients with partially damaged brain function. Traffic accidents and some surgeries have shown that the destruction of specific locations in the brain is linked to impairments in hearing and vision, for example. Consequently, we now know that the cerebrum contains different regions responsible for specific functions.

Several pieces of evidence indicate that the regions of the brain that govern human intelligence and personality are located in the frontal lobe. The most famous piece of evidence comes from a young railroad construction foreman named Phineas Gage. In 1848, a dynamite explosion accident blasted an iron rod 3 cm in diameter and 1 m in length into Gage's skull, piercing his frontal lobe and causing massive injury. After the accident, although he was physically healthy, his personality changed completely. Prior to his accident, he had been respected as an incredibly energetic, tenacious, capable, sharp man. However, his brain injury left him impulsive, stubborn, depressive, indecisive, and completely incapable of planning.

For several decades from the 1950s onward, about 50,000 people underwent lobotomy procedures, surgeries that involve removing the frontal lobe. Lobotomies were performed on psychiatric patients with pronounced excitability or anxiety in a time when antipsychotics did not exist. The surgery caused many patients to lose motivation, interest in the outside world, and concentration, in addition to hindering patients' abilities to reason and do things according to a plan. Thus, the important functions that maintain personality were proven to be concentrated in the frontal lobe.

Recently, functional magnetic resonance imaging (fMRI) has made it possible to identify cell groups in the brain that activate in response to stimulation. Functional MRI data has demonstrated the sites that activate in response to external stimuli (vision, hearing, etc.) and thought, supporting the idea that different sites in the brain are responsible for different functions.

Analysis of savant syndrome has produced even more astounding findings. A person with savant syndrome is intellectually disabled overall but possesses much greater capacity than an average person in a certain function, such as memorization or artistic ability. A classic case of savant syndrome concerns a patient who had memorized *The History of the Decline and Fall of the Roman Empire* word for word and could even recite it in reverse: from end to beginning.

Some people with savant syndrome are born with it, whereas others develop it after birth. Analysis of patients with savant syndrome has demonstrated the importance of communication between the left and right sides of the brain. Damage to the corpus callosum, the line of communication between the two sides of the brain, excessively expands partial function in the right side of the brain, resulting in an overall loss of integration. However, it appears that individual functions expand. Thus, although the division of functions among individual regions is important, so is the role of the pathways that integrate these individual regions.

However, it must be noted that these brain damage experiments only reveal the overall function of parts of the brain—they do not show all of the underlying components. The same goes for gene knockout mouse experiments that produce remarkable results. How can we unravel the necessary and sufficient conditions for the establishment of the mind?

The Principles of Brain Activity

Brain activity is extraordinarily complex and executes advanced functions. Therefore, many people previously believed that special principles that support cranial nerve activity might exist. The genetic recombination discovered in the immune system, which many thought might occur in brain cells as well, sparked relevant research. However, there have not yet been any brain activity-related discoveries that transcend conventional basic principles of life science.

In extremely general terms, there are three basic principles of brain activity. The first principle is that brain activity transmits information via electrical signals. Most neurons have long protrusions called "axons," some of which extend 1 meter or longer in humans. Information is transmitted through these long axons by means of an ion-driven electric current. The lipid bilayer that covers neurons is an insulating layer; the proteins that allow ions to pass through this bilayer (ion channels) produce an ion current, resulting in an electrical change called an "action potential" that proceeds down the axon at speeds as blisteringly fast as 430 kph (120 m/s) or as slow as 2 kph (0.6 m/s).

The second principle of brain activity is that electrical signals are converted to chemical signals in synapses, 20- to 30-nanometer (1 nanometer = 10^{-9} meters) junctions between neurons. In synapses, molecules called "neurotransmitters" are released from nerve endings. Electrical signals are converted into a chemical signaling format through which the receptor of the next cell will receive them. Of course, chemical signaling in synapses is far slower than electrical signals. However, with this transduction in synapses, nerve signals can be used respectively as excitatory or inhibitory signals, thereby enabling sophisticated regulation.

The third key principle of brain activity is that brain cells, of which there are said to be 10 billion to 100 billion, mutually form stable circuits. Cortical circuits feature two characteristics: a layered structure from the surface to the deep layer, and the formation of small, 0.5-millimeter-wide functional units called "columns." Opinions differ on whether circuit formation is determined completely by genes or whether circuits are reconstructed through the learning process after birth. At the very least, analysis of the central visual pathway in chickens shortly after birth suggests that external stimuli after birth select the neural pathways that will be used and therefore retained; the unused pathways are eliminated. Furthermore, in anatomically fixed circuits, research indicates that a mechanism that changes signal conduction at some synapses has associations with memory. A typical example of this phenomenon is long-term potentiation of synaptic transmission, where certain molecular changes enable more efficient signaling in repeatedly used synapses. Long-term potentiation is considered to be the molecular basis of memory.

The Brain's Information Processing

Without question, electrical signals are the basic mechanism of neural activity. The problem is the need for a mechanism that "recognizes" the signals transmitted. A mechanism to "store" signals is also necessary. Yet another mechanism is necessary for "comparative recognition," through which stored signals are retrieved as needed and compared with new signals. This series of mechanisms is collectively referred to as the brain's protocol of "information processing."

This perspective has been used as a framework in attempts to determine the principles of the brain's information processing by recreating it as an information-processing machine similar to a computer. These attempts are not necessarily based on the anatomical circuits of the brain. Rather, the typical approach is to construct a mathematical model that determines the extent to which the results of information processing reflect recognition and behavior in the brain, feed the input into an information-processing machine, and verify the extent to which biological phenomena are recreated.

Another approach to delineating the brain's mechanisms for information processing involves simulation based on molecular information elucidated from the perspective of molecular biology and known neural circuits; this simulation determines which molecules and synaptic activity in circuits can recreate partial brain function. Today, this field of research is called "systems biology." Researchers successfully used this approach to construct a model of cerebellar motor control.

Both of these approaches must be used in concert to get to the heart of the major questions regarding the brain.

The Relation Between Circuits and Function

As I stated earlier, circuit formation (determining which cells are connected to which) is absolutely critical to the basic functioning of the brain. From this perspective, an American research team considered it necessary to create a wiring diagram for all cells in the brain. In order to do so, the group is planning a large-scale project comparable to the sequencing of the human genome.

Experiments have also used a device called a "brain-machine interface (BMI)," which involves retrieving signals from the brain and using them to move a robotic device. With a BMI, when an electrode is inserted into a certain number of cells selected randomly from a specific region of the brain, the signals retrieved from the electrode can elicit nearly the same activity as that region of the brain. Thus, the brain's neural circuits overlap remarkably; it remains undetermined whether each neural network has specific, necessary roles.

Brain imaging research previously consisted primarily of visualizing external input in different regions of the brain. BMIs, which are in a sense a step forward from this previous research, attempt to expand the signals from various brain regions mechanically and link them to functions. As our understanding of brain function itself progresses, BMIs enable patients with motor dysfunction to move mechanical prostheses by using their thoughts, thus potentially bringing a medical boon and drawing great interest.

What to Ask in Order to Understand the Mind

So, how thoroughly can this extensive brain research help us understand the human mind? Life science ultimately elucidates only general principles; it is practically impossible for life science to tease out the dynamics of specific individuals. Even if we reach an understanding of the mechanism of susceptibility to diabetes, for example, we should interpret the mechanism as a matter of probability. Everyone has their own mind. The day may come when the general principles of psychological cognition (how the mind is formed in the sense of establishing the self) come to light. However, it is impossible to know what exactly an individual's mind holds. For example, there are plenty of question marks surrounding whether brain science is useful for predicting a person's economic behavior. When asking what the mind is, we must first define what there is to know and approach the question that way.

The Future of Life Science

In tracing the recent revolutionary progress of life science, I have discussed how life-science research has affected our worldview. The greatest object of intellectual curiosity left to humanity in the twenty-first century is the origins of the universe. Our curiosity about the universe stems from the desires to trace the origins of matter in our world and know whether the universe has an end. Our curiosity is perhaps equally powerful in regard to our inner selves: what are we, and how does life come to be? Humanity will always apply its wisdom in order to answer these two great questions.

The History of Life Science

Until the nineteenth century, biology consisted almost entirely of observation and description. In the twentieth century, analytical methods at last made their way into life science. In particular, biochemical analytical methods have yielded major results through the chemical analysis of metabolism and biological matter. These methods eventually solidified the material foundation of life science by determining the structure of DNA and the genetic code. In the latter half of the twentieth century, the new discipline of molecular biology emerged and gave researchers the unshakable conviction that these technological innovations would enable life science to comprehend the functions of life at the molecular level.

Today, it is thought that all genetic information has essentially been discovered. The human body contains more than 20,000 genes, which are translated into proteins; in turn, these genes—via RNA splicing—produce several times that many proteins, which undergo numerous modifications. There are said to be 10,000 to 100,000 carbohydrate chain modifications alone. Because of these modifications and others, such as phosphorylation, acetylation, and methylation, the ultimate number of proteins is staggeringly vast. In addition, proteins form complexes with each other and low-molecular-weight metabolites, and the interactions between these numerous molecules means that no two cells—even if they are the same type—are ever under completely identical conditions. The state of every individual cell is different, even if all the cells are lymphocytes. Scientists presume the same, or very close to the same, to be true of brain cells as well.

Based on the above concept, it is ultimately a bit dubious that a long succession of attempts to reduce life science to individual molecules or grasp the overall picture of an organism from the genetic level would naturally bring the overall picture to light. These combinations give life an astounding degree of complexity, which go far beyond the 10^{13} cells in the human body, potentially reaching 10^{20} combinations easily.

Life science has grown by leaps and bounds thanks to the analytical power of physics and chemistry. However, if we focus too much on analysis at the narrow level of the properties and functions of individual molecules, we risk losing sight of the integrated end result. The question of how an organism maintains its function as an individual, which researchers had previously tackled with a reductionist approach, now demands a big-picture approach—the most important orientation of life science. There are two approaches in life science research: a biomolecular chemistry approach, which views life science in terms of molecules, and a physiological approach, which views biology in terms of major regulatory or control systems. Developments in both approaches will determine the direction of life science in the twenty-first century.

Knowledge of Life Has a Profound Effect on Society

The fundamental question of life science is, in the end, "What is living?" This question is impossible to answer succinctly. In this chapter, I have introduced the principles behind the wide variety of strategies that organisms have developed over the course of evolution to survive, as well as the significance of those principles. In addition, life science strives to understand only general principles; as I have stated, the question of how individual organisms live is not the domain of life science.

Knowing the mechanisms of life is not only the starting point of inquiry in life science but will also likely affect society as the insights find applications in all the workings of humanity. As I explained earlier, if developments in brain science can illuminate the principles of human behavior, memory, and judgment, they can obviously have profound effects on educational policy, the structures of education and economics, and the makeup of society. Unraveling the mechanisms of living would unravel the causes of illness, advance the development of treatments, and illuminate measures for preventing disease. These developments in turn would likely have major effects on the demographics of society, the optimal allocation of healthcare costs, and other aspects of politics and economics.

Thus, learning the principles of life science is essential for understanding human society. Therefore, life science should be made a mandatory subject for all university students, including those in the humanities. In fact, Harvard University has already done so.

Solving Global Problems

The practical aspect of life science, which attempts to use organisms to solve the global problems facing humanity, will likely draw greater attention in the twenty-first century. As the recent financial chaos made clear, the problems plaguing humanity today are too great to be solved by any one country alone. Other examples include problems in securing oil and other scarce resources, problems associated with global warming, and problems related to food security. These issues have reminded us once again of how substantial a role life science plays in the contexts of food, energy, and the environment—the foundations of human survival on earth.

Life science has brought us various technological developments to help us deal with these problems. I would like to discuss one such development here: the practical application of genetically modified plants and microbes. When you consider the problem of food security on a global scale, the application of genetically modified organisms (GMOs) has the potential to save millions of people from starvation. However, many people around the world refuse to accept the use of GMOs.

As for problems related to energy, it is only a matter of time before the world's oil resources dry up. Therefore, renewable energy has attracted interest. As one example, genetically modified (GM) microbes that use cellulose or other plant components as substrates can already be applied to produce forms of energy such as alcohols and diesel fuel. In addition, it is essential to expand the use of GM microbes to the production of primary materials for chemical engineering.

Why do some people not accept the use of GMOs? There are two arguments against GMOs. The first is the difficulty in ensuring the safety of consuming GMOs as food. However, many people in the United States have been consuming GM foods such as corn and soybeans for over 20 years, and not a single specific safety issue has ever occurred. Scientific tests conducted according to international standards have yielded no evidence that any currently available GM foods have negative effects on the human body. Any scientific test of safety examines whether the test subject poses a significantly higher danger than something else; it does not prove that the subject poses no risk at all. Therefore, GM foods are considered safe because they demonstrate almost no difference with non-GM foods in the potential danger posed by consumption.

The second argument against GMOs centers on their environmental effects. According to this argument, plants produced by artificial genetic recombination will reproduce to such an extreme degree that they could negatively affect their ecosystems. However, although GMOs have already been cultivated extensively, no GMO has ever demonstrated this sort of property. The seeds of GMOs are exported around the world as grain and have been scattered everywhere in the process of transport, but there have been no instances of overgrowth. Furthermore, sterility can be introduced into GM plants to prevent them from overgrowing.

Although the technology for genetic recombination is new, the phenomenon itself has occurred repeatedly throughout the natural world ever since the dawn of organisms. Even today, the exchange of genes between different species of bacteria is not rare.

Conventionally, varieties of crops have improved by propagating the plants for several generations and selecting individual plants that demonstrated advantageous traits. Genetic modification is merely a technology that dramatically shortens this process.

Although GMOs are scientifically safe, some people feel uneasy about them. I feel that we need to promote further improvement and effective use of GMOs to open a new horizon for humanity's future and solve global problems. Of course, no one can be forced to eat GM foods—or any other food, for that matter. However, it is important to create a state of affairs in which eating GM foods is advantageous scientifically (high nutritional value), palatably (taste), economically (affordability), and politically (assurance of food security).

Rather than being seen as an issue for a single country, GMOs should be viewed as a solution to a global problem, and the directions in which the use of and research on GMOs are taken should be decided accordingly. All countries should work together to find a solution as they forge a clear strategy, obtain consensus, and establish accountability.

The Future of Humanity as Organisms

The idea about life that I want to emphasize most in this chapter is the principle of evolution. Evolution holds that life expresses astounding diversity by using limited genes within a unique, gene-based framework; that these genes themselves change dynamically; and that the species that exist today were born within interactions between genes and the environment. To put it simply, a solid understanding of the principles of Mendelian inheritance and Darwinian evolution is the shortest path to understanding "the principle of life."

Individuals as organisms will eventually die. We must also mentally prepare for the day when humans as a species will die. Many difficulties stand in the way of humanity carving out a future as organisms. It is completely impossible to predict how much humanity as a species will be able to adapt to future changes in the environment. Conversely, in regard to how each of us will complete our lives, life science has much to teach us. As I have said before, striving for eternal life is foolhardy. What matters is living our limited lifespans as productively and fully as possible.

What we can learn from life science is that a way of living that enables us to feel happy is itself compatible with how life should be. It would be ideal to spend one's entire life in a state of happiness. Realistically, however, it is impossible for everyone to be happy at all times. In more cases than can be cited here, people who have pursued the type of happiness that results from the fulfillment of desire have instead brought unhappiness not only to those around them but also to themselves. The other type of happiness is the elimination of anxiety; as I have stated, one method for achieving this type of happiness is religion. However, when religion's role becomes excessive, it restricts the intellectual activity of humanity and thus deviates from its role. Concepts such as intelligent design, which holds that all species as they exist today were created by God, are completely at odds with life science. In addition, the question of whether some higher power was at work at the birth of the universe is not one for science to answer. For example, the hypothesis that amino acids, the origin of life, fell to earth from space is gradually gaining acceptance. However, to think of this event as the work of some greater entity is unscientific.

With our remarkably developed cortical function, the curiosity of humanity will undoubtedly continue to develop in the two directions I described at the beginning of this section. Science, which is the pursuit of curiosity, needs to realize that there are limits to human activity. Although there is room for the optimistic viewpoint that humanity will be able to know everything through scientific progress, it is important to consider whether this knowledge would lead to true happiness. We must recognize that science and religion have their respective roles and their respective limits and that both lead to different facets of human happiness through different methods.

Biomedical Science Research
in Society

The Place of Life Science Today

Chapter 3 was a relatively abstract discussion. In this chapter, however, I would like to talk concretely about understanding the mechanisms of life and the structure for giving the benefits of that understanding back to society.

Back in the 1950s, when I was a university student, people saw life science as the most primitive of the natural sciences. Even all these years later, I still vividly remember physics majors in my year sarcastically telling me how nice it was that I was devoting my life to a backward discipline like life science. Although it was somewhat of an excuse, I countered that life science was only "backward" because physics and chemistry—which provide the methodologic foundations necessary for analyzing the molecules and cells that give rise to the complex phenomenon of life—had simply not advanced far enough.

Actually, those exchanges were happening right at the time when life science was progressing from its nineteenth-century origins of observation and classification into an increasingly concrete conceptualization of genes, leading to the discovery of the structure of DNA in the 1950s. That was when biology as a true science was born.

From that point onward, life science has made dramatic leaps forward through myriad technological innovations that seemed unimaginable in the 1950s: recombinant DNA technology, gene disruption, DNA sequencing technology, advancements in microscopes, and advancements in protein structure analysis. Thanks to these technological developments, it would not be an exaggeration to say that life science is the most attractive discipline in academia today.

The progress has ushered in a heyday of so-called reductionist methods that break life down into components and analyze their functions one by one. The possibility of understanding life at the molecular level, which was once little more than a dream, has become reality. Now, more than 50 years later, I fondly recall how my retorts in the face of those physics majors' taunts were actually not stuff and nonsense after all.

The major challenge awaiting life science today is how to reconstruct the results of reductionist factor analysis obtained from technological advancements and apply them to organisms, which are organic complexes. Furthermore, a clear path for specifically conducting research to address this issue has yet to emerge. To put it succinctly, life science today is in an era of transition from analysis to integration.

Between Life Science and Healthcare

The rapid development of life science has directly linked the long-standing, simple research question of "what life is" to the question of how to cure illness. The boundary between life science and medical science has disappeared.

In a narrow sense, medical research is research for curing diseases in humans. However, we obviously learn the principles of life from animal models and can then apply them to humans. Healthcare is the application of medical science to sick people (patients) in the real world; in other words, healthcare is the social implementation of medical science. We now live in a time in which life science develops into medical science and then into healthcare in an essentially integrated manner.

Currently, the Japanese government is looking to make a surefire return on its investments by pouring resources into projects that seek to link life-science research to the development of pharmaceuticals and medical devices. This trend has become pronounced in the last 10 years, particularly as a result of the incorporation of national universities, and the pattern of research investment has changed significantly. It seems that the government is making investments in research and development in pursuit of rather hasty returns.

Every researcher wants the fruits of advances in life science to be given back to society. However, in practice, things are not that simple.

As I discussed in Chapter 3, death comes for everyone. Everyone also wants to live a long, healthy life. There is no more powerful social need than that. Responding to the needs of society is certainly the role of the government. However, it is unlikely that government can meet the overarching social need for longer, healthier lives by investing as much as possible solely into areas with the most potential for drug development.

Why is this unlikely? Perhaps it is because many of the people who help shape policy on science and technology lack a sufficient understanding of what life science is, operating on the assumption that academia proceeds in the same way as the massive chemical plants and heavy industry that have long driven the development of Japanese capitalism.

In physics and chemistry, once basic principles have been determined, their future implementation can be predicted to a certain extent. For example, once the plans for a project to build a space probe like Hayabusa come into place, people can use the knowledge and technology available today to determine facets of the design: what sorts of missions to send it on, how big to make it to complete those missions, how much rocket propulsion to use, and how to craft the mechanisms for collecting information and control. The available technology then provides the means for applying new research and devices to unresolved portions, thereby propelling the project to completion.

However, in life science, no one can come up with that sort of design when launching a project to cure a disease. For example, despite the US government's War on Cancer, an Apollo Project-level undertaking, a review of the project years after its launch concluded that it was largely a failure. Several decades later, the United States has launched a new project to conquer cancer via immunotherapy. With concrete principles having already been discovered and their applications verified, this new project seeks to improve and refine these applications.

In life science, it is difficult to execute a project that intends to cure some disease within a certain timeframe. Why? Even if the project planners understand the core principle of life science—namely that the deciphering of the genetic code leads to the transcription of RNA, which is then translated into proteins with various functions—comprehending that fundamental concept is still worlds apart from understanding the mechanisms of life.

As I discussed in the previous chapter, this enormous gulf in understanding stems from the massive complexity, diversity, and hierarchy in life science.

Rough calculations suggest that humans have approximately 20,000 genes, each of which is transcribed. However, the transcribed RNA does not correspond exactly to its source gene. Instead, each RNA transcript is an edited version in which various meaningful regions (exons) of the source gene are linked together in different combinations. In this way, perhaps 10 or more different RNAs can be generated from each gene. Moreover, this estimated number of genes includes only those genomic regions that produce proteins or have some other purpose. However, researchers have discovered large numbers of molecules containing as-yet-undetermined information in regions previously thought to be meaningless; the number of these molecules nearly equals the number of genes in the human genome.

Furthermore, a translated protein also undergoes various modifications such as phosphorylation, acetylation, and glycosylation and then assembles with multiple other proteins to form a functional molecule. Thus, the power of combinations is at work in proteins. At the modification stage, it is not hard to imagine that diversity is added, roughly on the order of 10^2 to 10^4 combinations of functional molecules.

In addition, these basic elements are not necessarily expressed uniformly in all cells. Different types of cells, such as muscle cells, liver cells, and immune cells, are clearly differentiated in terms of the genes used and not used. The known mechanisms for the regulation of gene expression include DNA modification, methylation and acetylation of DNA-bound proteins called "histones," proteins that bind to gene expression regulation sites and modifications of those proteins, and a phenomenon in which products of gene expression feed back into gene expression. At this level, it would be no stretch to estimate a resulting complexity on the order of 10^4 to 10^5 gene expressions.

Understanding this diversity becomes an even bigger challenge when one accounts for the fact that the enzymes resulting from the above gene-expression process metabolize low-molecular-weight compounds, amino acids, carbohydrates, and fats in the body. The number of low-molecular-weight compounds in the body, even by conservative estimates, is in the tens of thousands. In addition, these metabolites form complexes with proteins that act on gene expression and metabolic control.

One could easily posit that this diversity is different for each of the 10^{13} cells in the body. For example, gene expression in immune cells differs completely depending on whether the cells are activated or not. This diversity is nearly impossible to quantify. Even the roughest estimate puts this diversity on the order of 10^{20}, which is not at all surprising. Do the dynamics of each individual cell have significance, or is there some pointless redundancy? We do not know.

However, this astounding hierarchy creates a multi-layered safety device, and a mechanism equipped with such a device truly recapitulates the nature of life. I have no idea when artificial intelligence will help unlock the mysteries of life phenomena; for now, these types of endeavors remain little more than wishful thinking on the part of information scientists. Artificial intelligence might offer a substitute for a meager fraction of biological function, though.

Therefore, in organisms, which have so many indeterminate factors, it is impossible to know what abnormalities will trigger what sorts of diseases without investigating them. In many cases, trial and error is necessary to determine how to cure a disease when a given abnormality occurs.

However, this does not mean that life-science research is pointless. I believe that what gives life science its identity is the high degree of chance it inherently involves; by no means is life science a "designed" science. Therefore, I feel that life science should investigate possibilities as broadly and diversely as it can. These far-reaching investigations will produce unexpected discoveries that will eventually lead to seeds in healthcare. In addition, new control theories will also influence information science.

PD-1, which my laboratory discovered, is now the main target of cancer immunotherapy and has whipped pharmaceutical companies around the world into a frenzied research and development war. When we discovered PD-1 in 1992, it was purely by chance. At the end of six to seven years of research, we learned that PD-1 is a negative immune system regulator, and we believed that it could be applied to cancer treatment. Through sheer serendipity, PD-1 is now applied in clinical settings, as I have already described in Chapter 2.

There are virtually innumerable examples of life-science research starting out attempting to elucidate some principle rather than curing some disease but, through major developments, making a crucial contribution to the treatment of a disease. At the same time, I also believe that of all the cases throughout history in which large sums of money have been invested in projects attempting to cure a specific disease, few have produced anything particularly noteworthy.

Social Implementation of Medicine and Life Science

I have already discussed how diversity and hierarchy are defining character-istics of life science. However, applying life science to humans in the form of medicine brings in yet another level of diversity. This extra level of diversity comes from the fact that every single person has a different set of genes.

In addition, every single person has a different environment and different lifestyle habits, as well as a different natural and cultural climate, depending on where they live. The field of medicine—itself an extension of or even inextricably linked with life science—must take that individuality into account.

The practice of medicine involves a physician dealing with and treating a patient as an individual. The therapy that worked for Patient A may not work for Patient B, and a given side effect that did not occur in Patient A may occur in Patient B. Dealing with patients as individuals means con-fronting these problems. In addition, the significance attached to medicine in a given society depends on that society's institutions, environment, and culture. For example, abortion is not uncommon in Japan. However, it needs to be recognized that there is fierce religious objection to abortion around the world. In addition to these social elements, doctors' decisions must also consider the wishes of the individual patient and the state of their disease.

In this context, doctors are charged with a role that goes well beyond that of a mere medical technician. Figuratively speaking, doctors deal with all four of the universal sufferings in Buddhist teaching: birth, aging, illness, and death. In addition, because physicians deal with patients as individuals, each of these problems requires its own particular solution rather than a general solution.

With perceptions now holding life science and medicine to be an integrated whole, it is vital that people recognize and understand the particularity of medicine, and we must strive for harmony between the health of individuals and society.

Investment in Medical Research

As I have already discussed, Japanese government funding of life-science research is now largely "exit-oriented" (aimed at immediate use). Due to various national strategies and other factors, a large percentage of research funding goes to project-style research that leads to something tangible and specific.

However, PD-1—a life-science discovery that came about by chance—took a different path. First, PD-1 was discovered in 1992. The next milestone was the development of a successful cancer therapy targeting PD-1 in an animal model, which came in 2002. Then, anti-PD-1 antibodies were approved for use in humans in 2014. Thus, it took a total of 22 years for PD-1 research to produce something "useful" and contribute to society.

If investments funded only the "useful" portions of long-term research, like the work that took place on PD-1, I fear that Japanese seeds would instantly shrivel up—Japan would become a limp, underdeveloped life-science nation in the blink of an eye.

Actually, when I was on the Japanese government's Council for Science and Technology (2006–12), the country's science and technology budget was ¥4–5 trillion (USD41.7–52.1 billion),[1] with roughly ¥200 billion (¥189.5–263.3 billion [USD1.97–2.74 billion] including increases associated with fund establishment) going to Grants-in-Aid for Scientific Research; of that roughly ¥200 billion, approximately 30% went to life science (Figure 1). In contrast, the United States dedicated roughly 60% of its science and technology budget toward life science across that same period. Furthermore, responsible for coordinating all of the US funding was

---

1 The USD figures in this paragraph were calculated by using an exchange rate of 96 JPY/1USD, the average annual exchange rate for 2006–12 (according to a Bank of Japan time series data search).

Figure 1. Comparisons between Japan and the United States regarding research funding for life science

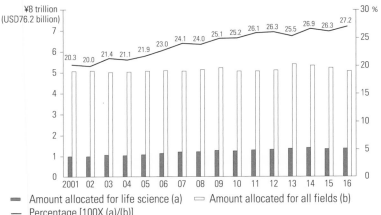

■ Amount allocated for life science (a)   ▭ Amount allocated for all fields (b)
— Percentage [100X (a)/(b)]

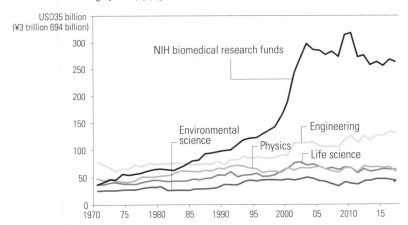

(Top) Funding for life-science research in Japan has remained nearly unchanged since 2001. The amount shown includes universities and other non-profit organizations or public institutions.
This figure was produced by the Ministry of Education, Culture, Sports, Science and Technology of Japan by using 2002–2018 data from the Statistics Bureau of Japan, Ministry of Internal Affairs and Communication.[2]
(Bottom) In the United States, funding for medical research accounts for a large percentage of the total.

This figure has been modified with permission from R&D Budget and Policy Program, American Association for the Advancement of Science. 2019. "Trends in Federal Research by Discipline, FY 1970–2017." https://www.aaas.org/sites/default/files/2019-06/Disc-1.jpg. American Association for the Advancement of Science.

2   This figure reflects an exchange rate of 105JPY/1USD, the annual average for 2001–16.

a single entity—the National Institutes of Health (NIH)—whose diligent watch oversaw investments to institutions nationwide, not only for medical research but also for basic life-science research.

Just recently, I had the opportunity to congratulate and visit with 2018 Japan Prize laureate Professor Max Cooper. He is famous for having identified B cells and discovering the phenomenon of class switching in the immune system. Now in his mid-80s, he is a great mentor and longtime friend.

His research focuses on the rearrangement of antibody and T-cell receptor genes in lampreys, which tell us how the immune system was reborn as the acquired immune system during the course of evolution. Dr. Cooper's research is quite unlikely to immediately lead to the development of pharmaceutical agents. However, because NIH grants can now be extended for five years, he plans to continue his research into his 90s.

When I look at Japan, I unfortunately cannot identify any entity that provides research funds with a similarly consistent, broad perspective that encompasses everything from basic life-science research, such as Dr. Cooper's work, to exit-oriented efforts such as the development of pharmaceuticals.

In 2015, an organization called the Japan Agency for Medical Research and Development was founded. This agency was touted as the Japanese version of the NIH; however, just as its name implies, it is an agency for funding medical research with a focus on exit-oriented development. Two additional funding agencies in Japan—the Japan Science and Technology Agency and the Japan Society for the Promotion of Science (JSPS)—generally provide funding for basic life science. There is no institution that integrates these agencies to steer life science as a whole in the same direction.

During my time on the Council for Science and Technology, a type of command center for science and technology policy, the organization issued a Science and Technology Basic Plan: a large framework that involved all science and technology, including life science, and underwent reviews every five years. However, in the fifth Science and Technology Basic Plan, which was issued in 2016, life science was dropped completely. As a result, life science in Japan may be rudderless. The system itself, it would appear, has collapsed.

As I have already said, the discovery of basic biological phenomena in microbes often leads to drug development. The most well-known example is the CRISPR-Cas9 gene editing system, which emerged from research on microbes and is now an important tool for researchers. Virtually every field in biomedical science now benefits from CRISPR-Cas9 technology; the tool has already found widespread application in the development of livestock products, for example.

Other developed countries see biomedical science in an integrated manner and pursue broad-ranging basic life-science research. However, when I look at Japan's warped, exit-oriented approach, I cannot help but feel that the future of Japanese life science is in great danger.

Competition in Biomedical Science Research

Biomedical science is a rapidly developing field that is constantly yielding new findings. Much in this field remains unknown.

In contrast, fields such as physics, especially particle physics, proceed differently. Problems are fairly well laid out; many people have the same sense that solving a given problem will unlock the next development, and people create and experiment with powerful equipment capable of solving the problem at hand. This problem-solving takes the form of joint research, an arrangement where a single paper might include hundreds of authors. Thus, what propels science is not so much competition as it is cooperation, although I dare say that competition occurs in the form of countries seeing who can produce the optimal equipment first. However, from my point of view, this level of competition is mostly meaningless. I think it would be enough for different countries to work together to create a single type of equipment.

In comparison, biomedical science, with its enormous diversity, requires originality—the ability to sniff out where something might lie hidden. Individual scientists must launch their own unique research based on where their own sensibilities point them or as they develop new methods.

The problem is that even this level of research requires large sums of funding. All of the necessary equipment, such as DNA sequencers, cell sorters, metabolomic analysis instruments, and microscopes, is now more expensive than it was when I began my research. Research funds of a few million yen (tens of thousands of dollars) would not be enough even if various analyses were outsourced.

For the record, life-science research in Japan clearly receives less funding than life science in the United States. Because funding for life-science research is scarce, competition for the resources is incredibly fierce. In addition, the number of researchers is increasing, emerging countries such as China are catching up, and it seems that the amount of data required to get a paper published is an order magnitude greater than it was 10 years ago.

Due to these circumstances, many young biomedical science researchers face enormous pressure to get published in a high-profile journal so that they can receive large amounts of funding and survive. Appearing in a leading publication should not determine survival, however. Of the papers published in leading journals, 80% are unlikely to be read by anyone 10 years later, and more than half may later be perceived to be incorrect. I personally do not see any significance in simply being published in a high-profile journal. However, many people worldwide are unable to judge a paper's merit for themselves, consequently often placing more importance on the name of the journal carrying the article than on the content of the paper itself.

There is a serious problem within this environment: the falsification of research. The pressure on researchers is so great that they sometimes resort to acts that destroy the reliability of their own data, which is career suicide. Some foolish researchers dabble in fraud, assuming that their schemes will go unnoticed for years and years. The fact that so many researchers find themselves in such desperate corners that they falsify their work is a serious problem.

From 2004 to 2006, I served as director of the Research Center for Science Systems, which is involved in designing the system for the JSPS's Grants-in-Aid for Scientific Research. I immediately proposed a reform of the Grants-in-Aid system.

Back then, the budget for Grants-in-Aid ranged from ¥155–161 billion (USD1.38–1.44 billion), which went to basic research in all fields. I proposed increasing the budget to ¥500 billion (USD4.46 billion), setting the grant amount for a single application in predetermined increments of ¥30–100 million (USD268,000–893,000), and reducing the number of applications so that reviews could be more thorough. Funding amounts should vary according to the needs of a given field, of course, so it would obviously be a mistake to review all fields on the same criteria and allocate funds accordingly. My proposal, which primarily concerned biomedical science, was not well-received. A recently enacted reform seems to have made things worse.

The reform in question concerns the Grant-in-Aid for Specially Promoted Research, a year-long grant of roughly ¥100 million (USD909,000)—the highest amount offered—awarded annually to approximately 10 research projects across all fields. I myself received this funding for many, many years, and it allowed me to pursue all kinds of research. However, the recent reforms for Grants-in-Aid have made it so that an individual researcher can now receive this funding only once in their lifetime. I immediately wrote a letter of protest to the JSPS, but of course I received no reply. Incidentally, the NIH's standard R01 grants are worth USD250,000 (¥27.5 million) apiece—enough for the implementation of a single project.

If Grants-in-Aid are to shoulder the development of biomedical science in Japan, they must provide research funding on a level that supports research based on beneficial competition and constructive assessment, and we must create an environment in which funding is available to large numbers of researchers working on diverse areas of basic biomedical science.

During the proofreading stage of this book, the government announced that the budget for the upcoming fiscal year would increase funding for Grants-in-Aid by ¥11–15 billion (USD100–136 million)—the first increase in 10 years. While this is truly good news, it also shows how much the Grants-in-Aid system needs reform.

Enhancing the Public's Understanding of Biomedical Science

Readers may be unfamiliar with the matters I have discussed thus far. If the public thoroughly understood the characteristics of biomedical science research, its significance, and its connection to society, support for biomedical science research might finally come alive.

In Japan, donations from the public make up a smaller percentage of research support than in other countries. The United States, in particular, is home to a mechanism by which patient-advocacy groups for various diseases can contribute to research on the corresponding diseases by raising vast amounts of donations and launching foundations to use those contributions for research funding. Establishing a similar system in Japan would require enhancing the public's understanding of research progress, current difficulties related to research, and ways to move research forward.

Of course, it is also important for researchers to appeal to the public directly. This is why Professor Yamanaka Shinya stepped up to raise funds for the Center for iPS Cell Research and Application at Kyoto University. However, researchers can only do so much on their own to appeal to society at large. Using my Nobel Prize money and the patent royalties due to me for the drug Opdivo, I established the Tasuku Honjo "Yuh-Shi" Fund at Kyoto University to cultivate young researchers. The fund has already received numerous donations, for which I am grateful.

I have long thought that science journalism in Japan needs major change. Over the past several decades, I have spoken with many science journalists, but unfortunately, very few of them had a sufficient understanding of what they were covering. Even worse, not only were these journalists not specialists, they were entirely new to the field; I have lost count of how many newspaper reporters have come to ask me questions despite confessing that they had been on the police beat until the previous year, when they were suddenly thrust into covering medicine.

This lack of qualified science journalists in Japan has had all kinds of harmful effects. The biggest problem is misreporting, which arises when journalists buy whole-heartedly into one-sided hype and claims without adequately assessing them. Due to the closed nature of the Japanese press, along with its lack of internationality and scientific judgment, the journalistic community is a major obstacle to nurturing the Japanese public's understanding of biomedical science. Classic examples include the coverage of stimulus-triggered acquisition of pluripotency (STAP) cells and the human papillomavirus (HPV) vaccine.

Let us look at the STAP cell debacle from a few years ago. The scandal shook the world; led to the resignation of Noyori Ryoji, the President of RIKEN (the major Japanese scientific research institute that oversaw STAP cell research); and drove Sasai Yoshiki, a coauthor of the STAP cell manuscripts, to take his own life. Why did this scandal occur? Shortly after the STAP cell manuscripts were published, I wrote a review in which I noted major flaws and expressed skepticism. However, Japanese TV and newspapers failed to even acknowledge the inconsistencies in the reported data and instead all breathlessly reported that STAP cells were a huge discovery because they offered an easier way to reprogram cells than the process for iPS cells did. If newspaper reporters had covered STAP cells in a level-headed, objective way, I am certain that this ugliness would not have occurred. There should have been no reason for Noyori Ryoji to resign. More than that, there should have been no reason for a tragedy like the loss of Sasai Yoshiki, a capable Japanese researcher. Such a tragedy must never happen again.

Later, a major problem occurred in the opposite direction with the HPV vaccine. The vaccine was found to be effective worldwide, and there was no definitive evidence regarding serious side effects. However, some people loudly complained of psychiatric disorders and other unspecified impairments resulting from the vaccine. As the media unilaterally ran with these claims, the coverage effectively brought the administration of the HPV vaccine in Japan to a halt. The very notion of altering a prevention-related medical policy in a developed country without definitive scientific evidence is outrageous. In fact, the HPV vaccine is so effective and widely used that the World Health Organization passed a resolution advising Japan to resume its use. Although the Japan Society of Obstetrics and Gynecology and the Japan Pediatric Society expect the Japanese government to resume recommendations regarding HPV vaccination soon, the media has never even hinted at admitting any fault. How truly unfortunate.

I can cite a personal experience as well. When I was on the Council for Science and Technology, government funding was earmarked for a Phase III clinical trial as part of a cancer vaccine project. The trial was the final assessment of drug efficacy, which is typically conducted by a pharmaceutical company. Phase I and Phase II trials assess safety with a small number of participants (typically 20 to 100). If these trials indicate efficacy, the drug advances to a Phase III trial, which involves a larger number of participants (typically 100 to 300). If a cancer vaccine demonstrates efficacy in a Phase

II trial, no pharmaceutical company will hesitate to invest large sums of money in the vaccine. However, the proposal to use government funding for this particular Phase III trial emerged through political machinations, and I vehemently opposed the proposal. The Japanese press vilified me, saying that I had unscrupulously opposed funding for such valuable research in my official capacity. This experience made me realize how incredibly important it is to improve the Japanese press's understanding of scientific content.

It is my earnest wish for the public to have a deeper understanding of science. My idea for making this wish come true is to cultivate science journalists who are independent of professional ties, in place of newspaper-affiliated science reporters, and for these independent science journalists to write articles on various newsworthy topics of interest.

I feel this way because biomedical science is extremely complex; it is not the sort of field that someone can comprehend in only a year or two and then write about effectively and appropriately. Perhaps it would be helpful to have more researchers who complete graduate school or a postdoctoral fellowship before pivoting to journalism and using their science knowledge to communicate findings to the public.

Thinking about the Future of Japanese Healthcare

The 21st Century Medical Forum

Healthcare comes to the general public as the product of basic medical research and clinical studies that develop from that research. While healthcare is the application of medical science, of course, it is also a part of social welfare. That interconnectedness means that drawing direct links between healthcare and medical science is not that simple. Even if medical research produces major results, those results cannot make their way back to the general public as benefits without the social infrastructure to support the application of those results in healthcare settings.

Although the Constitution of Japan guarantees its citizens the right to live in good health, this is extremely difficult to guarantee in practice. Fortunately, Japan has a universal health insurance system—National Health Insurance (NHI)—which is an outstanding social insurance system by global standards.

However, NHI is effectively bankrupt. Originally NHI was to maintain the public's health by using money collected as mutual aid. In reality, however, the system is currently maintained with tax money transferred from the government's general account.

The question of how to rebuild NHI is a core issue in the Japanese healthcare system today. As a representative of a voluntary association called the 21st Century Medical Forum, I have been thinking about this problem for a decade. In this chapter, I will discuss NHI based on Forum discussions. The Forum started in January 2009 with hopes of resolving problems in Japanese healthcare. By its tenth anniversary in 2019, the Forum had evolved into a healthcare reform advisory organization and healthcare policy think tank that offers solutions in forms such as expert panels, consulting, publications, seminars, and symposia.

Maintaining the National Health Insurance Program

The first defining characteristic of the Japanese healthcare system is that enrollment in health insurance is mandatory for all citizens. Furthermore, insurance premiums are based on income—a system that reflects a truly social, mutual spirit.

In addition, everyone enrolled in health insurance can visit any hospital they want; this free access is a unique feature of Japanese health insurance compared with the rest of the world. In Europe, public insurance systems generally designate a healthcare facility that people must visit first; if a person then requires treatment at a more advanced healthcare facility, a physician instructs the person how to proceed.

In Japan, healthcare fees are set according to a point-based official price system determined by the Central Social Insurance Medical Council, which comprises representatives from the government, insurance companies, patient advocacy groups, and medical and pharmaceutical companies. In addition, the Central Social Insurance Medical Council determines prices for drugs covered by insurance on a fee-for-service basis. Public insurance coverage is also expanding to cover more and more advanced healthcare.

These three major characteristics of NHI each have benefits and drawbacks.

First, I will use the American and European healthcare systems for the sake of comparison. In the United States, the Affordable Care Act (also known as "Obamacare") allows people to receive certain basic healthcare. However, most people enroll in health insurance through private insurance companies, which designate the healthcare facilities that their clients can visit, meaning that there is almost no free access. In addition, insurance premiums are typically quite high. Thus, healthcare in the United States centers on private rather than public insurance. In contrast, Europe has public health insurance; however, there is generally no free access. Public insurance fundamentally covers standard healthcare, whereas advanced healthcare is the domain of private insurance.

The Japanese health insurance system is extremely convenient and beneficial for patients. However, the system enables patients to go "hospital-hopping" to various healthcare facilities. In addition, patients often converge on university hospitals and other large hospitals, resulting in major problems such as doctors not having enough time to see patients.

The fee-for-service system is in danger of becoming a breeding ground for overtreatment, compared with a flat-fee system for the treatment of individual diseases. With a flat-fee system, healthcare providers can increase their revenue by performing the most efficient medical treatment for patients with a condition such as diabetes. However, the fee-for-service system creates a contradiction: inefficient treatment leads to higher revenue.

Changes in the Healthcare Environment and Associated Issues

The greatest problems facing NHI are demographic changes (such as the country's declining birthrate and aging population), attendant changes in the prevalence of major diseases, and yearly increases in healthcare costs due to medical advances. Due to the aging of the national population, healthcare costs will inevitably continue to rise.

The Japanese health insurance system is a so-called "pay-as-you-go" system that involves a transfer of income between generations. Specifically, the younger generations shoulder the healthcare costs of the older generations. The reason for this system is that, on average, at least half of an individual's lifetime healthcare costs are incurred during the last three to five years of life. Thus, the overall aging of the Japanese population has cast doubt on the sustainability of NHI.

The question of how to sustain this ideal universal healthcare system is a national issue. Naturally, solving this issue requires keeping healthcare costs in check, which the Japanese government is attempting to do by revising the healthcare-fee system that I described earlier. However, this revision has exacerbated two problems on the healthcare-provider side: deterioration of hospital management and a shortage of doctors. In addition, some patients are finding it more difficult to access healthcare equally and receive the same standard care as other patients.

Of course, there are loud calls for healthcare providers to determine how to manage hospitals more efficiently, allocate doctors appropriately, and reduce unnecessary care. Healthcare providers receive all sorts of advice on these points.

As for problems on the patient side, there is the element of moral hazard: patients rushing to university hospitals for minor issues like colds and visiting multiple hospitals to receive medication, for example.

We Japanese should be proud of NHI. To maintain it, we must forge a new, society-wide consensus and enact reforms based on that shared awareness to create a Japanese model of an insurance system suited to a super-aged society. Discussions at the 21st Century Medical Forum have generated proposals for such reforms, which focus on three major issues.

The first major issue is the need to reassess therapies, pharmaceuticals, medical devices, and tests. In the effort to allocate limited healthcare resources more effectively, these reassessments would make sure that health insurance does not provide any needless services or cover anything ineffective. Personally, I believe the ideal system is a mixed-billing system in which standard healthcare services are covered by public insurance and any healthcare services beyond those are paid out-of-pocket (by private insurance). The main point of this proposal is for public insurance to cover standard healthcare for everyone.

The next major issue is the rebuilding of community healthcare systems. Healthcare for people aged 75 and older is a major policy issue. The emphasis on this issue is driving measures such as comprehensive general assessments of patients, improvements in home care, coordination between medical-care/nursing-care services and discharge support, and work on end-of-life care support systems. These measures may be able to establish a new Japanese model of elderly care supported by community healthcare.

The third major issue is the need to reform the healthcare provision and consultation system. Patients who visit a major hospital without a referral already need to pay a certain amount of healthcare costs out of pocket at the current stage. The point of this feature is to encourage patients to first visit a local clinic, where a physician can determine if the patient needs to visit a specialized healthcare facility and can also advise the patient on treatment.

This aspect of the healthcare system is closely linked with the question of how to allocate doctors appropriately. As the media has reported, the Japanese system for providing medical care is imbalanced. Doctors are concentrated in large cities, and hospital doctors are overworked. Meanwhile, doctors with private practices have relatively large amounts of free time, and regional core hospitals have too few doctors. The maintenance of elderly care requires measures to allocate healthcare resources in a unified, appropriate fashion at the prefectural level.

Is There Really a Shortage of Doctors?

To resolve the shortage of doctors, the Japanese government has gradually increased capacities at medical schools around the country. Over the last 20 years or so, medical schools have seen their enrollment slots increase by about 50%. However, there is still no consensus as to whether Japan has a shortage or a surplus of doctors. In a way, both opinions may be correct.

For example, in large cities such as Tokyo, there may already be too many doctors in proportion to the population. However, in core provincial prefectures such as Shizuoka, which has a population of 3.65 million, the number of doctors per capita is low. This shortage of doctors is especially conspicuous in and around the Izu Peninsula in eastern Shizuoka Prefecture. In addition, doctors are distributed unevenly not only by region but also by specialty; there are shortages of obstetrician-gynecologists and surgeons but there are sufficient numbers of ophthalmologists, dermatologists, and anesthesiologists. Thus, the uneven distributions of doctors in regions and specialties may be the biggest problem in the Japanese healthcare system.

Another problem is the imbalance between doctors who are in private practice and doctors who work in hospitals. In general, many public hospitals suffer from a shortage of doctors.

The debate on how to solve this problem is split according to quite fundamental differences in opinion. From my point of view, the Japan Medical Association espouses a deep-rooted sense of individual freedom in terms of allowing doctors to choose where they practice, how they practice (whether to open a private practice or work in a hospital), and what they specialize in. I do not think that guaranteeing this freedom is an absolute must for doctors providing treatment covered by public health insurance.

Some medical treatments are not covered by health insurance, and some doctors do not deal with insurance at all. However, treatment within a universal healthcare system is performed with a mandate from the public as part of the social-security system. Certain restrictions may be necessary for this system to function properly.

First, rather than doctors being completely free to choose their specialties, it is important to reduce uneven distributions of doctors by determining how many doctors are necessary in given specialties (internal medicine, surgery, dermatology, and ophthalmology, for example), establishing limits on the numbers of doctors in those specialties, and assigning doctors to various regions based on their populations.

Next, there is also the concept of "medical regions," which typically consist of entire prefectures; the total numbers of doctors and of doctors per specialty must be assigned according to needs on an area-by-area basis. Consequently, doctors are subject to certain restrictions when obtaining certification to provide treatment covered by health insurance.

However, it is necessary to consider this restriction of freedom from the perspective of the doctors forced to accept it. To address doctors' concerns about being unable to ever move away from the area where they first work and also maintain the process of educating doctors into excellent medical professionals, it is necessary to incorporate lifelong education and specialty training into their career paths when assigning them to specific locations and specialties. Achieving this goal requires cooperation among universities and other medical educational institutions, local governments, and prefectural medical associations to draft doctor assignment plans based on a thorough consensus.

In discussions at the 21st Century Medical Forum during 2016, I proposed that this professional organization of doctors should create a new professional organization that would bear the responsibility of supporting NHI by itself. In fact, I also proposed this idea to the Japan Medical Association. In March 2017, I chaired the Ishi no Dantai no Arikata Kentoiinkai (Ideal Physicians' Association Exploratory Committee) within the Japan Medical Association, which assembled several proposals, including mine.

When I was formulating the proposal, I had the Japan Federation of Bar Associations (JFBA) in mind. The JFBA has the power to expel members, and members expelled from the JFBA cannot open private practices. I thought that a similar system might work in the medical field. As a professional organization where the doctors performing insurance-covered healthcare services impose certain regulations on themselves, a medical association would be able to control the freedom of its members to choose where, what, and how they practice.

End-of-Life Care and Views on Life and Death

Particularly in an aging society, everyone is aware that they will die someday and needs to recognize that the question of how to die is as equally important as the question of how to live. The question of how to die concerns not only medical science and healthcare but all of society.

Although it is obvious that everyone will eventually die, the number of people who are aware of their own mortality and are mentally prepared for it is surprisingly low. In this era in which fairly large numbers of people live to the age of 100, every Japanese citizen needs to think ahead about how they will approach the end of their life.

Thinking ahead about one's final days is intimately related to the issue of end-of-life care. Healthcare expenses increase in old age; half of a person's lifetime healthcare expenses are incurred before the age of 70 or so, whereas the other half is incurred from age 70 onwards. Setting aside the issue of how long a person will live past the age of 70 (or if they will even live that long), most healthcare expenses are generally incurred at the end of life.

One reason for these high healthcare expenses late in life is that many patients who spend their final days in long-term care hospitals have not made arrangements for their own deaths and sometimes simply lie there breathing (or being forced to breathe). Naturally, these patients come to the ends of their lives in an unhappy state.

The solutions to this problem should not be top-down measures that the government or some other entity forces on people. Rather, the ideal solution would be for every citizen to understand that their life is finite and think about their own death while they are still in good health. In addition, a patient's right to self-determination in regard to end-of-life care needs legally guarantees.

Such a legal guarantee would address a major problem for doctors: for example, even when a patient says that they do not want to be put on a ventilator, the patient's family could later accuse the doctor of murder for not having used a ventilator. To prevent this sort of situation, everyone should prepare a living will so that they can speak for themselves, and there may need to be a legal mechanism to ensure that right.

Perhaps education on this view of life and death should actually begin when people are young. Unfortunately, in primary and secondary education, death is considered a taboo subject. Young people are not taught the meaning of death or given an opportunity to think about it. I fear that this lack of education about death may conversely be why people often choose suicide so readily.

Thinking about death also serves as an opportunity to think about the importance of life, which confers significance to illness, treatment, medical care, aging, the end of life, and caregiving—all of which come to be perceived as interconnected. Instead of a culture in which people fail to perceive this interconnectedness and suddenly find themselves hovering between life and death due to a major illness, Japan should have a culture in which people think about the meaning of health, elderly people sufficiently understand that they will die someday, and dying people's families acknowledge the significance of a peaceful and happy death. However, this sort of culture does not seem to have strong roots in Japan yet.

Specific instances in which the right to self-determination at the end of life are enshrined in law include the Leonetti Law in France (enacted in 2005) and the Rights of the Terminally Ill Act in Australia (enacted in 1995). Although a similar law was debated in the Japanese Diet at one point, the discussion did not delve into much depth.

A living will, which is essentially a proclamation of an individual's own mandate regarding the desire to use or refuse life support, would solve many problems. In today's society, the people who play roles in late-life considerations—not only doctors and nurses but also religious figures—might need to take a more proactive approach to addressing the manner in which a person wishes to end their life.

Unfortunately, there are currently many instances in which doctors perform potentially unnecessary healthcare to prolong life, which inflicts additional suffering on patients.

From Treatment to Prevention

As healthcare spending increases dramatically, particularly for the elderly, the most important thing for us as healthcare personnel and as citizens is to avoid getting sick. I doubt anyone would disagree. To put it another way, I feel that healthcare should shift its focus from treatment to prevention.

Japan has one of the world's foremost systems for personal health management. From maternity handbooks to health checks for students in elementary and junior high school (until age 14) and regular checkups at workplaces, the Japanese government vigorously collects personal health data.

However, once this information is collected, nearly all of it languishes in storage without ever being used. Instead, people should have access to their individual health histories in the form of what would equate to personal databases. People could then manage their health by comparing their current health status with their previous data. In addition, when someone gets sick, their doctor can use that person's data when advising them on how to recover.

Tracking a person's health status throughout their life (assembling their life-course data) is not all that difficult. In this age of "big-data analysis," assembling life-course data is quite feasible. I would definitely like to see the Ministry of Health, Labour and Welfare prepare lifetime health data for individual citizens.

Another important area of prevention-oriented medical research is genome-cohort studies. Thanks to rapid developments in gene-analysis techniques, an individual's genetic background, susceptibility to disease, and other such information can be analyzed as data based on their DNA information. However, because of an information deficit in life science itself, it is impossible to predict the health status of every individual. In addition, nearly all diseases occur due not to genetic factors alone but to a combination of genetic and environmental factors. Therefore, we have access to very few data that tell us what sorts of genetic factors predispose people to what sorts of diseases or in what types of environments those diseases are likely to develop.

Japan is now adopting a research technique that involves having tens of thousands of healthy people enroll in studies that track their genetic information and health information every three or five years, following up with them at 10 and 20 years, and aggregating information regarding each person's diet and environment with their genetic predispositions to assiduously examine what diseases likely will develop. These studies include the Hisayama Study, which is being conducted in Hisayama, Fukuoka; the Nagahama Project, which is based in Nagahama, Shiga; the Tohoku Medical Megabank Organization, which consists mostly of residents of Sendai, Miyagi; and a genome-cohort study managed primarily by Iwate Medical University.

Hopes are high that in the future, this research could help not only predict the occurrence of certain diseases based on regional disparities across Japan and individuals' genetic information but also point to methods for preventing those diseases. Similar research is in progress in the United Kingdom and northern Europe as well. All of these studies are assiduous, long-term efforts founded on a trusting relationship between local residents and medical scientists. Although the projects involve major challenges such as cooperation with the government authorities who preside over local residents, the fruits of the research would be beyond measure.

Although medical science has conventionally investigated the causes of diseases after they develop, the research just described would enable the investigation of people's health with a window to the future.

In addition, collecting people's health status data, starting with their genetic information, will lead to the development of a new academic field—human life science. In the past, most developments in life science have emerged by discovering things in animal models and then confirming them in humans. With the development of genetic cohort studies, however, we can finally learn what sorts of differences in health arise from differences in individuals' diverse genes, as well as the results of the interactions between individuals' genes and their environments.

Mouse experiments have typically used inbred mice to eliminate the effect of individual differences as confounding factors. However, the results of these experiments always differ greatly from observations in humans. Thus, when the results of genome-cohort studies come out, they will remind us that the large differences between individuals are a major factor contributing to the difficulty inherent in medical science.

The ultimate disease-prevention method would make full use of genome-cohort research and databases to enable individuals to learn about their own genetic information and use it as a basis to establish lifetime health plans. For example, if parents know that their child is highly likely to develop diabetes, they can manage their child's diet with that knowledge in mind; when the child grows up, they can act on their own to avoid foods and behaviors that would cause them to develop diabetes, thereby enabling them to live healthier lives.

In the future, people could carry a personal card with a microchip containing all of their health information. When someone visits a healthcare facility, doctors could use that information to advise the person on optimal treatment and approaches to healthy living.

Rather than heading to a healthcare facility after getting sick, then, people could use their own health plans to proactively seek advice from doctors and thus live an entire lifetime in good health. By doing so, people may be able to enjoy healthy lifespans without increases in healthcare expenses.

References

Akihito, His Majesty the Emperor of Japan. 2010. "Linné and Taxonomy in Japan: On the 300th Anniversary of His Birth." *Proceedings of the Japan Academy Series B Physical and Biological Sciences* 86(3): 143–146. https://doi.org/10.2183/pjab.86.143.

Alt, F.W., and Honjo T., eds. 2007. *AID for Immunoglobulin Diversity*, volume 94. Advances in Immunology. Academic Press.

Darwin, C., and L. Kebler. 1859. *On the Origin of Species by Means of Natural Selection, or, the Preservation of Favoured Races in the Struggle for Life*. J. Murray.

de Waal, F. 2006. *Primates and Philosophers: How Morality Evolved*. Princeton University Press.

Dobzhansky, T. 1973. "Nothing in Biology Makes Sense except in the Light of Evolution." *The American Biology Teacher* 35(3): 125–129. https://doi.org/10.2307/4444260.

Goldenfeld, N., and C. Woese. 2007. "Biology's Next Revolution." *Nature* 445: 369. https://doi.org/10.1038/445369a.

Honjo T. 1999. "Kofukukan ni kansuru Seibutsugakuteki Zuiso" [Biological Reflections on Happiness]. In *Hikaku Kofukugaku* [Studies on Comparative Happiness], edited by H. Nakagawa, 221–233. International Institute for Advanced Studies.

Imura H. 2000. *Hito wa Naze Byoki ni Naru no ka: Shinka Igaku no Shiten* [Why We Get Sick: What Evolutionary Medicine Has to Say]. Iwanami Shoten.

Kurokawa K., et al. 2007. "Comparative Metagenomics Revealed Commonly Enriched Gene Sets in Human Gut Microbiomes." *DNA Research* 14(4): 169–181. https://doi.org/10.1093/dnares/dsm018.

Marusawa H., Matsumoto Y., and Chiba T. 2007. "I Hatsugan Katei ni okeru Idenshi Hen'i no Seisei no Bunshi Kiko: Herikobakuta Pirori-kin Kansen ni yoru AID no Ishosei Hatsugen Yudo" [Molecular Mechanisms of the Production of Gene Mutation in the Process of Gastric Carcinogenesis: *Helicobacter pylori*-induced Ectopic Expression of AID]. *Jikken Igaku* 25(12): 1841–1844. Yodosha Company, Ltd.

Miyata T. 1996. *Me ga Kataru Seibutsu no Shinka* [What the Eye Tells Us about the Evolution of Organisms], volume 37. Iwanami Kagaku Library. Iwanami Shoten.

Monod, J. 1971. *Chance and Necessity: An Essay on the Natural Philosophy of Modern Biology*. Alfred A. Knopf.

Okazaki I., Muramatsu M., and Honjo T. 2003. "AID ni yoru Kotai Bunshi Tayoka no Mekanizumu" [The Mechanism of AID-induced Antibody Molecule Diversification]. *Japanese Scientific Monthly* 56(10): 1075–1079.

Okita K., Ichisaka T., and Yamanaka S. 2007. "Generation of Germline-competent Induced Pluripotent Stem Cells." *Nature* 448: 313–317. https://doi.org/10.1038/nature05934.

Pennisi, E. 2007. "Working the (Gene Count) Numbers: Finally, a Firm Answer?" *Science* 316(5828): 1113. https://doi.org/10.1126/science.316.5828.1113a.

R&D Budget and Policy Program, American Association for the Advancement of Science. 2019. "Trends in Federal Research by Discipline, FY 1970–2017." https://www.aaas.org/sites/default/files/2019-06/Disc-1.jpg. American Association for the Advancement of Science.

Statistics Bureau of Japan, Ministry of Internal Affairs and Communication. 1996. Statistics Bureau webpage "Survey of Research and Development." http://www.stat.go.jp/english/data/kagaku/index.html. Ministry of Internal Affairs and Communication.

Taguchi A., L.M. Wartschow, and M.F. White. 2007. "Brain IRS2 Signaling Coordinates Life Span and Nutrient Homeostasis." *Science* 317(5836): 369–372. https://doi.org/10.1126/science.1142179.

Takahashi K., et al. 2007. "Induction of Pluripotent Stem Cells from Adult Human Fibroblasts by Defined Factors." *Cell* 131(5): 861–872. https://doi.org/10.1016/j.cell.2007.11.019.

Tang, J., et al. 2018. "Comprehensive Analysis of the Clinical Immuno-oncology Landscape." *Annals of Oncology* 29(1): 84–91. https://doi.org/10.1093/annonc/mdx755.

Treffert, D.A., and G.L. Wallace. 2002. "Islands of Genius: Artistic Brilliance and a Dazzling Memory Can Sometimes Accompany Autism and Other Developmental Disorders." *Scientific American* 286(6): 76–85.

Toyama K., Amari S., and Shinomoto S., eds. 2008. *Nokagaku no Teburu* [The Brain Science Table]. Japanese Neural Network Society, supervising ed. Kyoto University Press.

Yamanaka S., and Takahashi K. 2006. "Kagaku Tsushin: Kagaku Nyusu. Bunka Shita Taisaibo Kara Jinko Banno Kansaibo o Sakusei—iPS Saibo no Kanosei to Kadai" [Science Dispatches: Science News. Induced Pluripotent Stem Cells Produced from Differentiated Cells—The Potential and Challenges of iPS Cells]. *Kagaku* 76(12): 1177–1179. Iwanami Shoten.

NOBEL PRIZE IN PHYSIOLOGY OR MEDICINE BANQUET SPEECH

Your Majesties, your Royal Highnesses, Excellencies, Dear Laureates, Ladies, and Gentlemen.

On behalf of Professor Jim Allison and myself, I wish to express our heartful appreciation to the Nobel Assembly at the Karolinska Institute and the Nobel Foundation.

Cancer has been the No. 1 cause of death during the last half-century. The trend is getting even worse as the average life span increases.

The concept of cancer immunotherapy was theoretically proposed by the Australian Nobel Laureate Sir Frank Macfarlane Burnet over sixty years ago, and since then, a large number of people have tried to apply it, but without success. This was probably because their efforts focused on pushing the accelerators of the immune system. Jim and I independently discovered that the reactivation of the immune system by blocking two major negative regulators, CTLA4 and PD-1, can cure a significant portion of cancer patients. Fortunately, our experiments in mouse models were successfully applied to humans. As a result, Jim and I have experienced many occasions that have made us feel well rewarded, such as meeting cancer patients who say their lives were saved by our therapies.

Cancer immunotherapy is possible because we have a highly sophisticated immune system called "acquired immunity," which can catch small changes in tumor cells. How could we develop such a sophisticated immune recognition system that employs gene rearrangement? The genetic rearrangement mechanism must have developed accidentally—probably about five hundred million years ago, when vertebrates evolved. Thereafter, it must have persisted through natural selection due to the advantage of surviving infectious diseases.

Considering that the chance of such mutation and selection must be unbelievably low, we human beings are all very fortunate.

Jim and I both know that the development of our discovery is just beginning, as currently only 20 to 30% of patients respond to the immunotherapy. Andy Coghlan and Dan Chen described our discovery as the cancer equivalent of penicillin, which gave rise to a whole generation of antibiotics that changed medicine, and consigned most previously fatal infections to history. We encourage many more scientists to join us in our efforts to keep improving cancer immunotherapy. We sincerely hope this treatment will reach far and wide so that everybody on our planet can benefit from this evolutionary gift for healthy life.

Jim and I acknowledge that we were selected for this highest of all scientific honors. We accept the distinction with our deepest gratitude—gratitude for the great institutions that have supported our work, for our many devoted and skilled coworkers, without whom our achievements would have been impossible, and, finally, for Alfred Nobel for his wisdom to institute the prize and the people of Sweden for a fantastic Nobel Week.

Thank you.

10 December 2018
Honjo Tasuku

EPILOGUE

This book, *Advances in Cancer Immunotherapy: From Serendipity to Cure*, is descended from two earlier books of mine: *Inochi to wa Nani ka: Kofuku, Genomu, Yamai* (What is Life? Happiness, the Genome, and Illness) (Iwanami Shoten, 2009), and *PD-1 Kotai de Gan wa Naoru: Shin'yaku Niborumabu no Tanjo* (Curing Cancer with Anti-PD-1 Antibodies: The Birth of the Drug Nivolumab) (Iwanami Shoten, 2016; available only as an e-book). Specifically, Part I of *Inochi to wa Nani ka* is included as Chapter 3 of *Advances in Cancer Immunotherapy*, whereas *PD-1 Kotai de Gan wa Naoru* appears in its entirety, with additions and revisions, as Chapter 2 of the current book. Chapters 1, 4, and 5 are new material, written specifically for *Advances in Cancer Immuotherapy*.

I could not have written this book without the help of many people.

First, I would like to thank Sakata Hideya, Executive Director of the 21st Century Medical Forum, for reading Chapters 4 and 5 of the manuscript and sharing his thoughts with me. I serve as the Forum's Representative Caretaker; Chapters 4 and 5 of this book are based on the results of my activities with the Forum's members over the course of 10 years. Unfortunately I do not have enough pages to name them all, but I would like to take this opportunity to express my gratitude to them.

Next, I would like to thank Tanaka Taro, editor of Iwanami Shoten's magazine *Kagaku* (Science), who worked with me on the two earlier books I mentioned as well as this current book. I believe *Advances in Cancer Immunotherapy* turned out the way it did thanks to his meticulous direction. I also thank Naganuma Koichi, editor at Iwanami Shoten, who was in charge of publication.

The text of my Nobel Prize banquet speech is included at the end of this book with permission from the Nobel Foundation.

I express my sincere gratitude to Waku (Nakajima) Yuka, a researcher in the Department of Immunology and Genomic Medicine, Kyoto University Graduate School of Medicine, for proofreading the original Japanese manuscript entirely by herself.

The research that I have participated in and described here has been supported through the years by multiple institutions in Japan and elsewhere. None of this research would have been possible without the assistance of my collaborators at other institutions, my dear colleagues from my laboratory's AID and PD-1 projects, and my laboratory's former members and secretaries. I am profoundly thankful to these people—all 600 or so of them.

April 2019
Honjo Tasuku

INDEX

Science and Technology Basic Plan,
130
COVID-19, and significance of science,
7–8
Crick, Francis, 72
CRISPR-Cas9 gene editing system, 131
crystallin molecules, origin of, 74–75
CTLA-4
    absence of, consequences, 44
    antibody-mediated blockade and
        cancer suppression, 44
    as an immune brake, 24, 30–32,
        43–44
    knockout mice, autoimmune
        responses, 48
    negative regulatory mechanism and,
        43–44
cytokines, 18–19, 24
    family of, 39–40
    inflammatory-response-triggering,
        production, 57
cytosine, 16, 75

mitochondrial, 96
and RNA, roles in evolution of life, 76
Dobzhansky, Theodosius, 67
dynamic fluidity, 77

HIV resistance, and CCR5 gene mutation, 101
Hodgkin lymphoma, anti-PD-1 antibody treatment, *33*, 35–36, 52
Hood, Leroy, 79
human genome *See* genome, human
human life science, field of, 147
human mind, and life science, 113–14
human papillomavirus (HPV) vaccine, media misinformation about, 134, 135

I

ICOS, accelerator molecules, 24
IgA *See* immunoglobin A
IgG *See* immunoglobin G
illness, conception of, 73
imatinib, 28, 106, *106*
immune activation, PD-1 negative regulatory factor, 44
immune brakes
  consequences of destroying, 32
  CTLA-4 preventing overactivation, 43–44
  discovery and understanding, 30–32
  disengagement by anti-PD-1 antibodies, effects, 25, 32
  PD-1 as, 24, 30–32, 47, 48
  release by PD-1 antibodies, 24, 25, 30–32, *31*
  transmission into cells, 46–47
immune cells
  atheromas, forming of, 25
  classes, 21
  definition, 18
immune function, and age, 108
immune memory, 89
immune response, T-cell regulation of, 42–43
immune surveillance, 30
  activation, 40, 44
  application (Burnet), 38
  neoantigen expression, 30, 39
  reactivation of, 30–32
immune system
  activation by cytokines, 39–40
  activation methods, 41

and aging, 25–26
anti-PD-1 antibodies and brain function control, 25
cancer involvement, 38
cells in, 24
dysregulation and inbred mice, 45
excessive activity, effects, 25
expression of antibody genes, 79–80
and gut bacteria, 95–96
ideal, 22–23
memory of, 90–91
and organism's survival, 99–100
reactivation of, 30–32
regulation model, 43–44
regulatory role, 26
response, activation and deactivation signals, 107
self and non-self, distinction, 22
immune tolerance, 30
  anticancer therapy hypothesis (Boon), 40
  antigens as triggers, 107
  brake application, 30–32
  concept, 39
  mechanism, 42–43
immunity *See also* immune brakes
  acquired, 18, 19
    and antibodies, 19
    characterization, 19
    evolution, 21–22
    and limited genetic information, 78
    principles, 19–22
    in vertebrate organisms, 90
  innate
    and acquired, difference, 22
    functioning of, 18–19
    mechanisms, 89–90
    post-infection, 88–89
    regulation of, 42–43
    types of, 18
immunogens, 107
immunoglobin A (IgA) antibodies, 20, 91
immunoglobin G (IgG) antibodies, 20, 91
immunological memory, 91

About the Author

Dr. Honjo Tasuku

Dr. Honjo was born in Kyoto in 1942. After graduating from the Faculty of Medicine, Kyoto University, and completing his doctorate at the university's Graduate School of Medicine, he went on to positions such as Fellow at the Carnegie Institution of Washington; Visiting Fellow at the National Institutes of Health in the United States; Assistant Professor of the Faculty of Medicine, University of Tokyo; Professor of the Faculty of Medicine, Osaka University; and Professor of the Faculty of Medicine, Kyoto University. He currently serves as Deputy Director-General and Distinguished Professor of the Kyoto University Institute for Advanced Study as well as Director of the Center for Cancer Immunotherapy and Immunobiology at Kyoto University Graduate School of Medicine. Dr. Honjo is a winner of the 2018 Nobel Prize in Physiology or Medicine.

Selected works:

Genomu ga Kataru Seimeizo: Gendaijin no tame no Saishin Seimei Kagaku Nyumon [The Image of Life as Told by the Genome: A New Introduction to Life Science for Today]. Kodansha, 2013.

Kofukukan ni kansuru Seibutsugakuteki Zuiso [Biological Reflections on Happiness]. Shodensha, 2020.

Men'eki to Ketsueki no Kagaku (Iwanami Koza Gendai Igaku no Kiso 8) [The Science of Immunity and Blood, volume 8. Iwanami Courses: Principles of Current Medicine], joint editor. Iwanami Shoten, 1999.

Seimeitai no Mamorikata (Iwanami Koza Bunshi Seibutsu Kagaku 11) [How Organisms Defend Themselves, volume 11. Iwanami Courses: Molecular Biology], editor. Iwanami Shoten, 1991.

Donations

We gratefully accept your donations through the following website.
Tasuku Honjo "Yuh-shi" Fund:
https://www.kikin.kyoto-u.ac.jp/en/contribution/nobel/

（英文版）がん免疫療法とは何か
Advances in Cancer Immunotherapy: From Serendipity to Cure

2021年3月27日　第1刷発行

著　者　　本庶 佑
訳　者　　アンドリュー・ゴンザレズ
発行所　　一般財団法人出版文化産業振興財団
　　　　　〒101-0051 東京都千代田区神田神保町2-2-30
　　　　　電話　03-5211-7283
　　　　　ホームページ　https://www.jpic.or.jp/

印刷・製本所　　大日本印刷株式会社